Managing Editor
Mara Ellen Guckian

Editor in Chief
Karen J. Goldfluss, M.S. Ed.

Creative Director
Sarah M. Fournier

Cover Artist
Sarah Kim

Imaging
James Edward Grace

Publisher
Mary D. Smith, M.S. Ed.

For correlations to the Common Core State Standards, see pages 105–106 of this book or visit *http://www.teachercreated.com/standards/*.

Teacher Created Resources
12621 Western Avenue
Garden Grove, CA 92841
www.teachercreated.com
ISBN: 978-1-4206-8082-9

© 2017 Teacher Created Resources
Made in U.S.A.

Table of Contents

Introduction

The *Minutes to Mastery* series was designed to help students build confidence in their math abilities during testing situations. As students develop fluency with math facts and operations, they improve their abilities to do different types of math problems comfortably and quickly.

Each of the 100 tests in this book has 10 questions in key math areas. Multiple opportunities are presented to solve the standards-based problems while developing speed and fluency. The pages present problems in a variety of ways using different terminology. For instance, in subtraction, students might be asked to *subtract* or to *find the difference*. Terms like *less* and *minus* are both used to ensure that students are comfortable with different phrasings. Word problems are included to provide additional practice decoding text for clues. Critical thinking and abstract reasoning play such an important role in solving math problems, and practice is imperative.

Keep in mind, timing can sometimes add to the stress of learning. If this is the case for your math learner(s), don't focus on timing in the beginning. As confidence in the process of answering a number of different types of questions builds, so will accuracy and speed. Then you can introduce timing.

Establish a timing system that works well for your group. Here are steps to help you get started:

1. Present a worksheet without officially timing it to get a sense of how long it will take to complete—perhaps 10 minutes. Ideally, you want all ten questions per page to be answered.

2. Allow students to practice using the preferred timer before taking a timed test.

3. Remind students to write their answers neatly.

4. Take a few timed tests and see how it works. Adjust the time as needed.

5. Work to improve the number of correct answers within the given time. Remind students that it is important to be accurate, not just fast!

6. Encourage students to try to do their best each time, to review their results, and to spend time working on areas where they had difficulties. The Tracking Sheet can be used to record the number of correct answers for each test. The final column can be used for the date the test was taken or for initials.

The section at the bottom of each page can be used to record specific progress on that test, including the time the student started the test, finished the test, the total time taken, how many problems were completed, and how many problems were correct.

Hopefully, with practice, all students will begin challenging themselves to go faster, while remaining accurate and writing clearly.

Tracking Sheet

Name _____

Numbers		
Test 1	/10	
Test 2	/10	
Test 3	/10	
Test 4	/10	
Test 5	/10	
Test 6	/10	
Test 7	/10	
Number Lines		
Test 8	/10	
Test 9	/10	
Addition		
Test 10	/10	
Test 11	/10	
Test 12	/10	
Test 13	/10	
Test 14	/10	
Test 15	/10	
Test 16	/10	
Test 17	/10	
Test 18	/10	
Test 19	/10	
Test 20	/10	
Test 21	/10	
Test 22	/10	
Subtraction		
Test 23	/10	
Test 24	/10	
Test 25	/10	
Test 26	/10	
Test 27	/10	
Test 28	/10	
Test 29	/10	
Test 30	/10	
Test 31	/10	
Test 32	/10	
Test 33	/10	
Test 34	/10	
Test 35	/10	

Multiplication		
Test 36	/10	
Test 37	/10	
Test 38	/10	
Test 39	/10	
Test 40	/10	
Test 41	/10	
Test 42	/10	
Test 43	/10	
Test 44	/10	
Test 45	/10	
Test 46	/10	
Test 47	/10	
Test 48	/10	
Division		
Test 49	/10	
Test 50	/10	
Test 51	/10	
Test 52	/10	
Test 53	/10	
Test 54	/10	
Test 55	/10	
Test 56	/10	
Test 57	/10	
Test 58	/10	
Test 59	/10	
Test 60	/10	
Test 61	/10	
Test 62	/10	
Test 63	/10	
Test 64	/10	
Mixed Operations		
Test 65	/10	
Test 66	/10	
Test 67	/10	
Test 68	/10	
Money		
Test 69	/10	
Test 70	/10	
Test 71	/10	
Test 72	/10	

Fractions		
Test 73	/10	
Test 74	/10	
Test 75	/10	
Test 76	/10	
Test 77	/10	
Test 78	/10	
Time		
Test 79	/10	
Test 80	/10	
Test 81	/10	
Test 82	/10	
Test 83	/10	
Test 84	/10	
2-D Shapes		
Test 85	/10	
Test 86	/10	
Perimeter		
Test 87	/10	
Test 88	/10	
3-D Shapes		
Test 89	/10	
Test 90	/10	
Area		
Test 91	/10	
Test 92	/10	
Measurement		
Test 93	/10	
Test 94	/10	
Test 95	/10	
Test 96	/10	
Test 97	/10	
Test 98	/10	
Charts and Bar Graphs		
Test 99	/10	
Test 100	/10	

Name _____ Date _____

Which numbers are in the *ones* place?

1. 34 _____ **2.** 607 _____

Write each number in word form.

3. 26 _____

4. 265 _____

Write the words as numbers.

5. nine hundred two _____

6. seven hundred fifty-five _____

Write the numbers shown by the base ten blocks.

7.

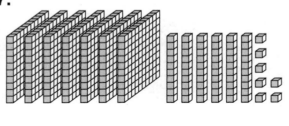

_____

8.

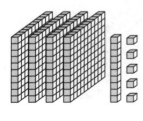

_____

Write the numbers shown by the abacus.

9.

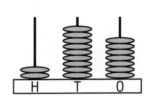

_____

10.

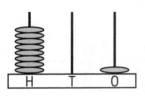

_____

Started:	Finished:	Total Time:	Completed:	Correct:

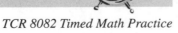

Name _____ Date _____

Which numbers are in the *tens* place?

1. 472 _____

2. 65 _____

Write each number in word form.

3. 346 _____

4. 89 _____

Write the words as numbers.

5. eight hundred forty-one _____

6. one hundred fifty-six _____

Write the numbers shown by the base ten blocks.

7.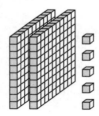

_____

8.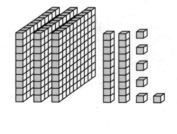

_____

Write the numbers shown by the abacus.

9.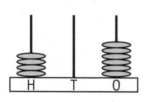

_____

10.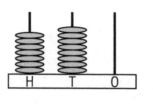

_____

Started:	Finished:	Total Time:	Completed:	Correct:

Name _____ Date _____

Which numbers are in the *hundreds* place?

    1. 572 _____

    2. 756 _____

Write each number in word form.

    3. 996 _____

    4. 893 _____

Write the words as numbers.

    5. nine hundred thirty-two _____

    6. two hundred seventy-five _____

Write the numbers shown by the base ten blocks.

    7.
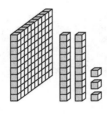

        _____

    8.
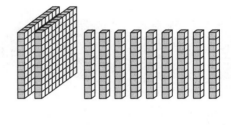

        _____

Write the numbers shown by the abacus.

    9.
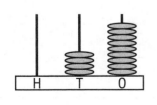

        _____

    10.
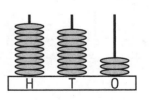

        _____

Started:	Finished:	Total Time:	Completed:	Correct:

Name _____ Date _____

Which numbers are in the *thousands* place?

1. 1,683 _____   **2.** 8,722 _____

Write each number in word form.

3. 1,999 _____

4. 3,048 _____

Write the words as numbers.

5. two thousand, five hundred sixty-seven _____

6. six thousand, two hundred ninety-six _____

Write the number shown by the base ten blocks.

7.

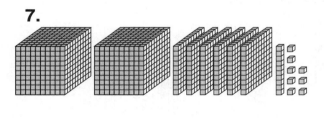

_____

8.

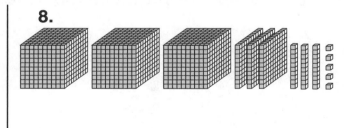

_____

Write the number shown by the abacus.

9.

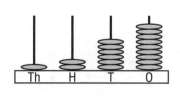

_____

10.

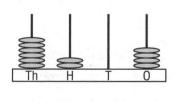

_____

Name _____ Date _____

A	B	C	D
Ants	**Beetles**	**Dragonflies**	**Butterflies**

Look at the groups of insects in the chart. Use the correct inequality sign, < or >, to make each statement true.

1. A ◯ B

2. C ◯ A

3. B ◯ C

4. C ◯ D

5. D ◯ A

6. B ◯ D

Use the correct inequality sign, < or >, to make each statement true.

7. 3,243 ◯ 3,423

8. 4,209 ◯ 4,290

9. 2,987 ◯ 2,978

Count the two groups of insects. Use the correct inequality sign, < or >, to make the statement true.

10.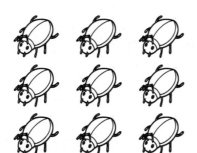

Started:	Finished:	Total Time:	Completed:	Correct:

Name _____ Date _____

Use the number line to solve problems 1–4.

1. 18 + 4 = _____   **2.** 25 − 15 = _____

3. 14 + 10 = _____   **4.** 30 − 7 = _____

Use the number line to find the numbers for problems 5–10.

5. Start at 15 and count forward 6.

     The number is _____.

6. Start at 25 and count forward 10.

     The number is _____.

7. Start at 20 and count forward 12.

     The number is _____.

8. Start at 22 and count forward 8.

     The number is _____.

9. Start at 32 and count backward 7. Then go forward 3.

     The number is _____.

10. Start at 35 and go backward 5. Then go forward 10.

     The number is _____.

Started:	Finished:	Total Time:	Completed:	Correct:

Name _____ Date _____

Use the number line to solve problems 1–4.

1. 10 + 10 + 5 = _____   **2.** 28 – 18 = _____

3. 10 + 5 + 7 = _____   **4.** 32 – 20 = _____

Use the number line to find the numbers for problems 5–7.

5. Start at 65 and count backward 20.   **The number is** _____.

6. Start at 55 and count backward 9.   **The number is** _____.

7. Start at 70 and count backward 12.   **The number is** _____.

Use the number line to find the numbers for problems 8–10.

8. Start at 20 and count forward 15.

     The number is _____.

9. Start at 40 and count backward 15. Then go forward 1.

     The number is _____.

10. Start at 25 and go backward 7. Then go forward 12.

     The number is _____.

Started:	Finished:	Total Time:	Completed:	Correct:

Name _____ Date _____

Find the sums. Look for sums of 10 to help add the numbers.

1.	7	2.	5	3.	8
	3		7		2
	+ 8		+ 5		+ 2

Solve each word problem. First, look for sums of 10 to find the answers.

4. There are 5 plums, 2 pears, and 5 bananas in the basket. How many pieces of fruit are in the basket altogether?

   _____ + _____ = 10 ⟶ 10 + _____ = _____

5. There are 4 cars, 5 vans, and 6 busses in the parking lot. How many vehicles are in the parking lot altogether?

   _____ + _____ = 10 ⟶ 10 + _____ = _____

6. Cody has 7 blue crayons, 9 red crayons, and 3 yellow crayons. How many crayons does he have altogether?

   _____ + _____ = 10 ⟶ 10 + _____ = _____

7. There are 6 pigs, 5 cows, and 4 horses in the barn. How many animals are in the barn altogether?

   _____ + _____ = 10 ⟶ 10 + _____ = _____

Circle the two numbers in each problem that equal 10. Then solve the problem.

8. $8 + 8 + 2 =$ _____

9. $7 + 3 + 9 =$ _____

10. $4 + 5 + 6 =$ _____

Started:	Finished:	Total Time:	Completed:	Correct:

Name _____ Date _____

Look at the models below. Use them to answer questions 1 and 2.

Ⓐ 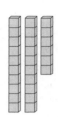   Ⓑ 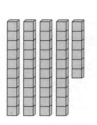   Ⓒ 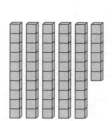   Ⓓ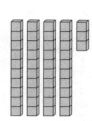

1. Which group shows 56?   **A**   **B**   **C**   **D**

2. Which group shows 26?   **A**   **B**   **C**   **D**

Count forward by tens to complete each sequence.

3. 10, 20, _____, _____, 50, _____

4. 110, _____, 130, _____, 150, _____

Count backward by tens to complete each sequence.

5. 90, _____, _____, 60, _____, 40

6. _____, 62, _____, 42, _____, 22

Complete the table below.

	10 Less	Number	10 More
7.		**30**	
8.		**55**	
9.		**83**	
10.		**22**	

Name _____ Date _____

Look at the models below. Fill in how many *hundreds*, *tens*, and *ones*.

1.

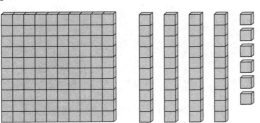

___ hundred   ___ tens   ___ ones

2.

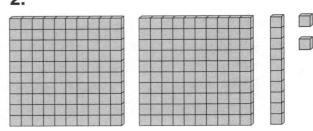

___ hundreds   ___ ten   ___ ones

Count forward by hundreds to complete each sequence.

3. 100, 200, _____, _____, 500, _____, 700

4. _____, _____ 500, _____, 700, _____

Count backward by hundreds to complete each sequence.

5. 777, _____, 577, _____, 377, _____

6. 600, _____, 400, 300, _____, _____

Complete the table below. Show 100 less and 100 more for each number.

	100 Less	Number	100 More
7.		650	
8.		230	
9.		190	
10.		670	

Started:	Finished:	Total Time:	Completed:	Correct:

Name _____   Date _____

Complete the number patterns.

1. 2, 4, 6, _____, _____, _____, _____

2. 1, 3, 5, _____, _____, _____, _____

3. 3, 6, 9, _____, _____, _____, _____

4. 4, 8, 12, _____, _____, _____, _____

5. 21, 23, 25, _____, _____, _____, _____

Look at the patterns below. Describe how each pattern works.

6. 1, 2, 4, 8, 16

_____

7. 5, 10, 15, 20

_____

8. 7, 10, 13, 16, 19

_____

9. 48, 24, 12, 6

_____

Continue the dot pattern below. Add 2 more sets of dots.

10.

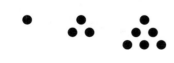

| Started: | Finished: | Total Time: | Completed: | Correct: |

Name _____   Date _____

Find the following sums.

1. $900 + 90 + 9 =$ _____

2. $500 + 40 + 8 =$ _____

3. $800 + 60 + 3 =$ _____

Write the value of each underlined digit.

4. 2<u>9</u>3 _____

5. <u>8</u>53 _____

6. 26<u>4</u> _____

Use the place value chart to expand the numbers.

7. 333

	H		T		O

8. 567

	H		T		O

9. 75

	H		T		O

10. 308

	H		T		O

Started:	Finished:	Total Time:	Completed:	Correct:

Name _____ Date _____

Write the greatest number possible using all the digits supplied.

1. 3, 2, 5, 6 _____

2. 2, 1, 3, 4 _____

3. 6, 7, 6, 2 _____

4. 9, 2, 5, 8 _____

Write the sets of numbers from *greatest* to *least*.

5.

4,634	4,246	4,433	4,334
_____	_____	_____	_____

6.

9,695	7,765	9,959	8,567
_____	_____	_____	_____

Write the sets of numbers from *least* to *greatest*.

7.

1,674	1,246	1,467	1,764
_____	_____	_____	_____

8.

7,865	8,765	7,856	8,567
_____	_____	_____	_____

Write the value of each underlined digit.

9. 8,8<u>8</u>8 _____

10. <u>3</u>,232 _____

Started:	Finished:	Total Time:	Completed:	Correct:

Name _____   Date _____

Add to solve each addition problem.

1. 2,000 + 400 + 30 + 2 = _____

2. 6,000 + 700 + 20 + 1 = _____

3. 8,000 + 400 + 60 + 7 = _____

Write the value of each underlined digit.

4. 2,<u>5</u>49 _____

5. <u>8</u>,316 _____

6. 7,6<u>2</u>8 _____

Find the following sums.

7.	6,000	**8.**	8,000	**9.**	5,000
	300		400		600
	60		20		40
+	7	+	3	+	7

What number is represented by the chart below? Write the number word.

10.

7	Th	9	H	5	T	1	0

Number: _____

Number Word: _____

_____

Started:	Finished:	Total Time:	Completed:	Correct:

Name _____ Date _____

Regroup and add these 2-digit numbers to find the sums.

1. 67
    + 44

2. 54
    + 38

3. 88
    + 52

Regroup and add these 3-digit numbers to find the sums.

4. 324
    + 586

5. 973
    + 637

6. 555
    + 487

Solve the word problems. Show your work.

7.	There are 789 students in Jenny's school and 453 students at her brother's school. How many students are there altogether?
	_____ students
8.	Sam has 47 blue marbles and 74 green marbles. How many marbles does Sam have altogether?
	_____ marbles
9.	Sally scored 23 points, Suri scored 14 points, and Sara scored 17 points. How many points did they score altogether?
	_____ points
10.	Jimmy hopped on one foot for 32 seconds on his first try, 48 seconds on his second try, and 59 seconds on his last try. How many seconds did Jimmy hop on one foot altogether?
	_____ seconds

Started:	Finished:	Total Time:	Completed:	Correct:

Name _____ Date _____

Try to solve the problems in your head.

1. 200 + 200 + 200 = _____

2. 300 + 400 + 300 = _____

3. 700 + 700 + 200 = _____

Circle the two numbers in each problem that equal 10. Then solve the problem.

4. 6 + 4 + 9 = _____

5. 8 + 9 + 2 = _____

6. 5 + 7 + 5 = _____

Which symbol will make each problem true?

| < | > | = |

7. 232 ◯ 223   **8.** 767 ◯ 776

Add the numbers on either side of the box. Then place the correct sign in the box to compare the two problems.

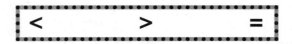

| < | > | = |

9. 3 + 4 + 3 = _____   [ ]   4 + 3 + 4 = _____

10. 10 + 6 = _____   [ ]   8 + 8 = _____

Started:	Finished:	Total Time:	Completed:	Correct:

Name _____　Date _____

Regroup and add 2-digit numbers.

1.　78
　　+ 43

2.　66
　　+ 44

Regroup and add 3-digit numbers.

3.　459
　　+ 372

4.　831
　　+ 579

Regroup and add 4-digit numbers.

5.　3,256
　　+ 5,955

6.　5,878
　　+ 3,249

Fill in the missing number to solve each problem.

7. $8 + 7 +$ _____ $= 20$

8. $6 + 4 +$ _____ $= 18$

Solve the word problems. Show your work.

9. There are 15 boys, 12 girls, and 2 teachers in the classroom. How many people are in the classroom?

_____ **people**

10. Jake knows that the bike he wants costs $350 and the helmet he wants costs $85. How much money does he need to save to buy both items?

$ _____

Started:	Finished:	Total Time:	Completed:	Correct:

Name _____   Date _____

Add each set of numbers to find the total.

1. $8 + 7 + 5 + 6 =$ _____

2. $3 + 3 + 3 + 3 =$ _____

3. $20 + 30 + 40 =$ _____

4. $100 + 60 + 8 =$ _____

Solve the addition problems.

5.
$$\begin{array}{r} 9 \\ 8 \\ 2 \\ +\ 5 \\ \hline \end{array}$$

6.
$$\begin{array}{r} 22 \\ 33 \\ +\ 55 \\ \hline \end{array}$$

7.
$$\begin{array}{r} 390 \\ +\ 469 \\ \hline \end{array}$$

Fill in the missing numbers to complete each problem.

8. $12 +$ _____ $= 18$

9. $60 +$ _____ $= 100$

Solve the word problem and show your work.

10.	Thirty-five chickens and seventeen ducks were in the barnyard. How many animals were in the barnyard altogether?
	_____ **animals**

Started:	Finished:	Total Time:	Completed:	Correct:

Name _____   Date _____

Find the difference for each problem.

1. $100 - 50 =$ _____   **2.** $14 - 7 =$ _____

Subtract the numbers to solve each problem.

3. $\begin{array}{r} 18 \\ -\ 9 \\ \hline \end{array}$ **4.** $\begin{array}{r} 18 \\ -14 \\ \hline \end{array}$ **5.** $\begin{array}{r} 19 \\ -\ 6 \\ \hline \end{array}$

Read each statement and solve the problem.

6. 9 take away 7 = _____   **7.** 12 take away 6 = _____

Solve each word problem. Show your work.

8.	Tarek's dog had 8 puppies. He gave 6 puppies to friends. How many puppies does he have left? _____ **puppies**
9.	Ella folded 12 towels. She put 8 towels in the closet. She put the rest near the bathtub. How many towels did she put near the bathtub? _____ **towels**
10.	There were 16 tomato plants in the garden. The twins picked all the tomatoes on 10 plants. How many plants still had tomatoes on them? _____ **plants**

Started: Finished: Total Time: Completed: Correct:

Subtraction

Name _____ Date _____

Write a number sentence to solve each problem.

1. [base-ten blocks] − [tens rod]

_____

2. [base-ten blocks] − [tens rod]

_____

Find the difference for each problem.

3. $17 - 9 =$ _____

4. $16 - 7 =$ _____

5. $12 - 6 =$ _____

6. $18 - 8 =$ _____

Use the three numbers to create two subtraction problems.

7. | 14 21 7 | _____ _____

8. | 19 3 22 | _____ _____

Circle the correct number sentence to solve each word problem.

9.	Sami has twenty-two dollars in her wallet. If she spends seven dollars at the fair, how much money does she have left?
	$22 + $7 = $29 $22 − $7 = $15 $7 − $22 = $15

10.	There were 100 bananas in the basket in the morning. By the end of the day the elephants had eaten 56 of them. How many bananas were left in the basket?
	100 + 56 = 156 100 − 44 = 56 100 − 56 = 44

Started: _____ Finished: _____ Total Time: _____ Completed: _____ Correct: _____

Name _____   Date _____

Use the number line to find the differences.

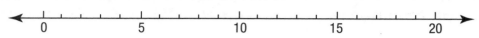

1. 16 – 11 = _____   **2.** 17 – 13 = _____

Write a number sentence for each set. Solve the problems.

3.

_____ **bells**

4.

_____ **flowers**

5.

_____ **kites**

Write and solve the problems.

6. Subtract 6 from 12. _____

7. Subtract 5 from 14. _____

8. Subtract 0 from 9. _____

Answer the questions.

9. What is four minus two? _____

10. What is 15 take away nine? _____

Started:	Finished:	Total Time:	Completed:	Correct:

Name _____ Date _____

Complete the number wheel. Start at the arrow and go clockwise. Rewrite each problem on the lines below the wheel. The first one has been started for you.

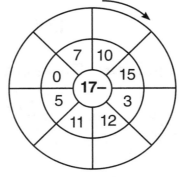

1. 17 – 10 = _____

2. _____

3. _____

4. _____

5. _____

6. _____

7. _____

8. _____

Solve the problems. Write each problem as a number sentence.

9.	Eric invited 19 classmates to his party and 14 were able to come. How many classmates missed the party?
	_____ – _____ = _____ **classmates**
10.	For his birthday, Eric received 14 presents. He opened five presents before everyone had cake. How many presents does he have left to open?
	_____ – _____ = _____ **presents**

Started:	Finished:	Total Time:	Completed:	Correct:

Name _____   Date _____

Read and solve the word problem. Show your work.

| 1. | Mrs. Jenkins bought 12 pumpkins. She gave 5 to her neighbor. How many pumpkins did she have left? |

_____ **pumpkins**

Rewrite the subtraction problems using numbers and solve.

2. sixteen minus seven equals _____

3. ten take away seven equals _____

4. fourteen minus six equals _____

5. thirteen take away eleven equals _____

Solve the subtraction problems.

6.   90
    − 85

7.   18
    − 15

8.   55
    − 46

Try to solve the following problems in your head.

9. $600 - 200 - 100 =$ _____

10. $250 - 200 - 25 =$ _____

| Started: | Finished: | Total Time: | Completed: | Correct: |

Name _____ Date _____

Solve the 2-digit subtraction problems.

1.   99
    − 35
     ‾‾‾‾

2.   79
    − 66
     ‾‾‾‾

3.   64
    − 34
     ‾‾‾‾

Fill in the blanks to complete each problem.

4. 22 − _____ = 11

5. 76 − 24 = _____

6. _____ − 45 = 10

7. 98 − 80 = _____

Change the addition problems to subtraction problems.

8. 3 + 9 = 12   _____ − _____ = _____

9. 15 + 6 = 21   _____ − _____ = _____

10. 12 + 6 = 18   _____ − _____ = _____

Started:	Finished:	Total Time:	Completed:	Correct:

Name _____ Date _____

Regroup to solve the 2-digit subtraction problems.

1. 44
   − 29

2. 62
   − 33

3. 55
   − 46

Find the missing numbers to complete each problem.

4. 6 5
   − ☐ 9
   ‾‾‾‾‾
     3 ☐

5.   9 ☐
    − 4 7
    ‾‾‾‾‾
      ☐ 1

6. 6 8
   − 4 ☐
   ‾‾‾‾‾
    ☐ 9

7. 5 7
   − ☐ 8
   ‾‾‾‾‾
    2 ☐

Change each addition problem to a subtraction problem.

8. 24 + 62 = 86 _____ − _____ = _____

9. 52 + 48 = 100 _____ − _____ = _____

Solve the word problem. Show your work.

| 10. | Jack has two jars of marbles. *Jar 1* has 85 marbles and *Jar 2* has 48 marbles. What is the difference between the two jars of marbles? |

| Started: | Finished: | Total Time: | Completed: | Correct: |

Name _____ Date _____

Count the base 10 blocks. Write the problem and solve.

1.   =   – _____

2.   =   – _____

3.   =   – _____

4. 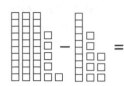   =   – _____

5. 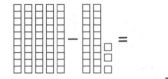   =   – _____

6.   =   – _____

Solve the word problems. Show your work.

7.	There were 45 children in the pool. Thirty-six children got out. How many were left in the pool?
8.	Michael counted 67 red cars. Ryan counted 48 red cars. How many more red cars did Michael count?
9.	Maddox read 45 books. Linn read 54 books. How many more books did Linn read?
10.	Julian saved $42.00. He needs $99.00 to go on a ski trip. How much more money does Julian need to save?

Started:	Finished:	Total Time:	Completed:	Correct:

Name _____ Date _____

Regroup to solve the 2-digit subtraction problems.

1.	21 − 9	**2.**	63 − 46	**3.**	31 − 18	**4.**	40 − 15

Complete the subtraction squares. Subtract rows and columns (not diagonals).

5.
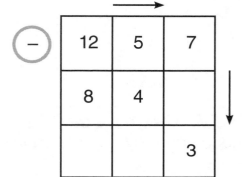

6.
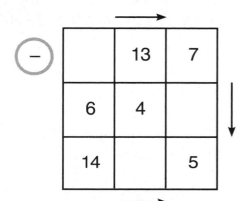

7.
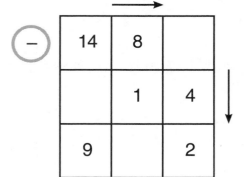

8.
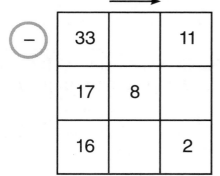

9.
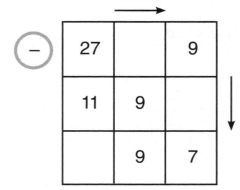

10.

Started:	Finished:	Total Time:	Completed:	Correct:

Name _____ Date _____

Solve the 3-digit subtraction problems.

1. 269 – 130	**2.** 564 – 153	**3.** 878 – 463	**4.** 397 – 255	**5.** 265 – 134

Solve the word problems. Show your work.

6. Shelley bought a new laptop for $850. How much change did she get if she gave the cashier $900?

7. Joey and his sister are saving for a new TV. They have saved $385 and the TV costs $489. How much more money do they need to save?

8. Colton is saving up for new shoes. He has $32 and the shoes cost $46. How much more money does he need?

Find the missing numbers to complete each problem.

9.
```
   6  6  7
 - 4 []  2
 [] 5  5
```

10.
```
   8  2 []
 - 4  1  6
   4 []  1
```

Started:	Finished:	Total Time:	Completed:	Correct:

Name _____ Date _____

Regroup and solve the 3-digit subtraction problems.

1.	300	2.	750	3.	523	4.	477
	− 51		− 476		− 135		− 399

Find the missing numbers to complete each problem.

5.
```
  8 □ 4
- 5 8 6
-------
  2 1 □
```

6.
```
  9 □ 4
- □ 2 5
-------
  5 6 9
```

7.
```
  5 4 □
- □ 9 8
-------
  3 4 8
```

Solve the word problems. Show your work.

8. Mrs. Francis bought 300 notebooks for her school.
She gave each of the 237 students a notebook.
How many notebooks does she have left?

_____ notebooks

9. Tam has saved $495 and Lori has saved $168.
How much more money does Tam have than Lori?

$_____

10. New team uniforms will cost $853. The soccer team earned $674.
How much more money do they need for their uniforms?

$_____

Started:	Finished:	Total Time:	Completed:	Correct:

Subtraction

Name _____ Date _____

Find the difference for each problem.

1. 19 – 10 = _____

2. 100 – 75 = _____

3. 29
  – 15

4. 56
  – 37

5. 487
  – 288

Find the missing numbers to complete each problem.

6. 13 – _____ = 4

7. 55 – 33 = _____

8. 200 – _____ = 150

Solve the problems. Show your work.

9. The farmer picked forty-nine bushels of apples. He took thirty-six bushels to the Farmers Market. How many bushels does he have left?

_____ **bushels**

10. There were 356 runners in the big race. Of these runners, 297 crossed the finish line. How many runners did not finish the race?

_____ **runners**

Started:	Finished:	Total Time:	Completed:	Correct:

Name _____ Date _____

Solve the following problems.

1.	49	2.	54	3.	586	4.	841
	− 27		− 38		− 372		− 652

Solve the money problem. Show your work.

5.	Mickey had $5.00 in his piggy bank. He lent his friend $2.89. How much money does he still have?

Write two subtraction problems that use the numbers in the box.

6. _____

7. _____

| 13 | 20 | 7 |

Write three number sentences that have a difference of 20.

8. _____

9. _____

10. _____

Name _____ Date _____

Write number sentences for each picture.

1. ★ ★ ★ ★ ★
   ★ ★ ★ ★ ★   _____ × _____ = _____
   ★ ★ ★ ★ ★

2. ★ ★ ★ ★ ★ ★ ★
   ★ ★ ★ ★ ★ ★ ★
   ★ ★ ★ ★ ★ ★ ★   _____ × _____ = _____
   ★ ★ ★ ★ ★ ★ ★
   ★ ★ ★ ★ ★ ★ ★

3. ★ ★ ★ ★ ★ ★ ★ ★ ★
   ★ ★ ★ ★ ★ ★ ★ ★ ★   _____ × _____ = _____

Circle the number sentence that represents the total number of stars.

4. ★ ★ ★ ★ ★ ★ ★ ★   **A.** $8 + 4 = 32$
   ★ ★ ★ ★ ★ ★ ★ ★
   ★ ★ ★ ★ ★ ★ ★ ★   **B.** $8 \times 4 = 32$
   ★ ★ ★ ★ ★ ★ ★ ★   **C.** $4 + 8 = 32$

Circle *true* or *false* to answer each of the statements.

5. 2×7 equals 7×2 **true**   **false**
6. 5×5 equals $5 + 5$ **true**   **false**
7. 4×5 equals 2×10 **true**   **false**

Write three multiplication problems that equal 24.

8. _____ × _____ = _____

9. _____ × _____ = _____

10. _____ × _____ = _____

Started: Finished: Total Time: Completed: Correct:

Name _____ Date _____

List the multiplication factors for the following numbers.

1. 6 _____

2. 17 _____

3. 15 _____

4. 16 _____

First solve the addition problems. Then write the addition problems as multiplication problems.

5. 3 + 3 + 3 + 3 + 3 + 3 = _____   _____ × _____ = _____

6. 7 + 7 + 7 + 7 + 7 + 7 + 7 = _____   _____ × _____ = _____

7. 9 + 9 + 9 + 9 + 9 = _____   _____ × _____ = _____

Use each picture to solve each problem.

8. × _____

_____ groups of _____ equal _____

9. × _____

_____ groups of _____ equal _____

10.

 × _____

_____ groups of _____ equal _____

Started:	Finished:	Total Time:	Completed:	Correct:

Name _____   Date _____

Complete the number sentences.

1. $7 \times 5 =$ _____

     $5 \times$ _____ $= 35$

2. $6 \times 2 =$ _____

     $2 \times$ _____ $= 12$

3. $3 \times 8 =$ _____

     $8 \times$ _____ $= 24$

4. $9 \times 7 =$ _____

     $7 \times$ _____ $= 63$

Find the products of these numbers.

5. 6 times 6 equals _____

6. 4 times 4 equals _____

7. 5 times 5 equals _____

Circle *true* or *false* to answer each of the statements.

8. 6×8 equals 8×6 **true**   **false**

9. 3×6 equals 2×9 **true**   **false**

10. 3×10 equals 5×7 **true**   **false**

Started:	Finished:	Total Time:	Completed:	Correct:

Name _____ Date _____

Solve the word problems. Show your work.

1. Mom arranged six vases of flowers. Each vase held seven flowers.
How many flowers did she use altogether?

_____ **flowers**

2. There are six bags of apples on the counter. Each bag holds four apples.
How many apples are there altogether?

_____ **apples**

Find the products of these numbers.

3. $8 \times 6 =$ _____

4. $3 \times 8 =$ _____

5. $7 \times 4 =$ _____

6. $9 \times 5 =$ _____

Find the factors that are missing to solve the multiplication problems.

7.
$$\begin{array}{r} 7 \\ \times\ \square \\ \hline 21 \end{array}$$

8.
$$\begin{array}{r} \square \\ \times\ 6 \\ \hline 18 \end{array}$$

9.
$$\begin{array}{r} 5 \\ \times\ \square \\ \hline 35 \end{array}$$

10.
$$\begin{array}{r} \square \\ \times\ 7 \\ \hline 49 \end{array}$$

Started:	Finished:	Total Time:	Completed:	Correct:

Name _____ Date _____

Find the products of these numbers.

1. 10
    × 4

2. 11
    × 5

3. 12
    × 6

Find two sets of numbers that equal the given number when multiplied.

4. 24 _____ × _____   _____ × _____

5. 12 _____ × _____   _____ × _____

6. 36 _____ × _____   _____ × _____

7. 40 _____ × _____   _____ × _____

Solve the problems. Write each problem as a number sentence.

8.	One cupcake costs 5 cents. How much will 7 cupcakes cost?
	_____ ¢
9.	There are seven students in Mr. John's class. He gave each student seven crayons. How many crayons did he hand out altogether?
	_____ **crayons**
10.	If one elephant has two tusks, how many tusks will 10 elephants have?
	_____ **tusks**

Started: Finished: Total Time: Completed: Correct:

Name _____ Date _____

Find the total number of objects in each set.

1. 5 groups of 6 fish = _____ **fish**

2. 9 groups of 4 flowers = _____ **flowers**

3. 6 groups of 8 balls = _____ **balls**

4. 4 groups of 7 stars = _____ **stars**

Use the base 10 blocks to find the totals.

5.   **9 groups of 10 = _____**

6. 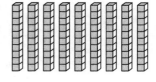   **4 groups of 10 = _____**

7.   **5 groups of 10 = _____**

Circle *true* or *false* to answer each of the statements.

8. 4×9 equals 3×12 true   false

9. 2×7 equals 3×4 true   false

10. 3×8 equals 4×6 true   false

Started:	Finished:	Total Time:	Completed:	Correct:

Name _____ Date _____

Find the products of these numbers.

1.　　9
　　　× 7

2.　　7
　　　× 8

3.　　8
　　　× 4

Write a multiplication number sentence to describe each model.

4.  _____

5. _____

6. _____

Find the missing number facts.

7. 2 × _____ = 22

8. 6 × _____ = 42

9. 5 × _____ = 25

10. 9 × _____ = 81

Started:	Finished:	Total Time:	Completed:	Correct:

Name _____   Date _____

Circle *true* or *false* to answer each of the statements.

1. $3 \times 7 = 7 \times 3$ **true**   **false**

2. $9 \times 4 = 5 \times 7$ **true**   **false**

3. $2 \times 9 = 6 \times 3$ **true**   **false**

4. $6 \times 5 = 3 \times 10$ **true**   **false**

Write the following addition problems as multiplication problems. Solve the problems.

5. | $6 + 6 + 6 + 6 + 6 + 6 + 6 + 6 + 6$ |

_____ × _____ = _____ or _____ × _____ = _____

6. | $4 + 4 + 4 + 4 + 4 + 4 + 4$ |

_____ × _____ = _____ or _____ × _____ = _____

7. | $9 + 9 + 9 + 9 + 9 + 9 + 9 + 9$ |

_____ × _____ = _____ or _____ × _____ = _____

Find the products of these numbers.

8. $\begin{array}{r} 7 \\ \times\,9 \\ \hline \end{array}$

9. $\begin{array}{r} 8 \\ \times\,8 \\ \hline \end{array}$

10. $\begin{array}{r} 8 \\ \times\,7 \\ \hline \end{array}$

| Started: | Finished: | Total Time: | Completed: | Correct: |

Name _____ Date _____

Write three multiplication problems that equal 36.

1. _____ × _____ = _____

2. _____ × _____ = _____

3. _____ × _____ = _____

Find the products of these numbers.

4. 9 × 12 = _____

5. 4 × 12 = _____

6. 8 × 11 = _____

Find the factors that are missing to solve the multiplication problems.

7.
```
      5
  × [   ]
  -------
     45
```

8.
```
  [   ]
  × 8
  -----
   64
```

9.
```
     11
  × [   ]
  -------
     33
```

10.
```
  [   ]
  × 7
  -----
   63
```

Name _____   Date _____

Find the product for each statement.

1. 5 times 11 = _____   **2.** 9 groups of 4 = _____

3. 5 times 7 = _____   **4.** 6 groups of 8 = _____

Find the factors that are missing to solve the multiplication problems.

5.
$$\begin{array}{r} \square \\ \times\ 7 \\ \hline 56 \end{array}$$

6.
$$\begin{array}{r} 8 \\ \times\ \square \\ \hline 32 \end{array}$$

7.
$$\begin{array}{r} 12 \\ \times\ \square \\ \hline 24 \end{array}$$

Solve the word problems. Show your work.

8.	Brent walked three miles a day for six days. How many miles did he walk altogether? _____ **miles**
9.	If you eat two bananas every day for one week, how many bananas will you eat? _____ **bananas**
10.	Eli wrote five valentines everyday for 10 days. Altogether, how many valentines did Eli write? _____ **valentines**

Started: Finished: Total Time: Completed: Correct:

Multiplication

Name _____ Date _____

Find the factors that are missing to solve the multiplication problems.

1.   2
    × ☐
    ‾‾‾‾
    18

2.   ☐
    × 7
    ‾‾‾‾
    42

3.   12
    × ☐
    ‾‾‾‾
    60

4.   ☐
    × 8
    ‾‾‾‾
    56

Use the pictures to solve each multiplication problem.

5. 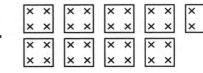   _____ groups of 4 = _____

6.   _____ groups of 4 = _____

7.   _____ groups of 4 = _____

Complete the number sentences using <, >, or = signs.

8. 5×5 ⬭ 6×4

9. 3×6 ⬭ 2×9

10. 5×7 ⬭ 9×6

Started:	Finished:	Total Time:	Completed:	Correct:

Name _____ Date _____

There are seven days in one week.

1. How many days are there in five weeks? _____

2. How many days are there in seven weeks? _____

3. How many days are there in 11 weeks? _____

Write two multiplication problems using the numbers in each box.

4.	9, 54, 6

_____ × _____ = _____ and _____ × _____ = _____

5.	7, 9, 63

_____ × _____ = _____ and _____ × _____ = _____

Find the products of these numbers.

6. $7 \times 4 =$ _____

7. $6 \times 8 =$ _____

8. $9 \times 4 =$ _____

Circle *true* or *false* to answer each of the statements.

9. $8 \times 6 = 7 \times 7$ true   false

10. $4 \times 4 = 8 \times 2$ true   false

Started:	Finished:	Total Time:	Completed:	Correct:

Name _____ Date _____

Find the products of these numbers.

1.	11 × 5	2.	4 × 6	3.	9 × 4

Complete the number sentences using <, >, or = signs.

4. 4×8 ◯ 3×11

5. 3×4 ◯ 2×6

6. 9×6 ◯ 5×7

Fill in the blanks to complete each multiplication problem.

7. _____ $\times 4 = 16$

8. $6 \times 8 =$ _____

9. _____ $\times$ _____ $= 56$

Solve the word problem. Show your work.

10. Josh got a new bookshelf that has four shelves.   He wants to put seven books on each shelf. How many books does he need?

_____ **books**

Started: Finished: Total Time: Completed: Correct:

Name _____ Date _____

Divide each set of objects into equal groups. State how many groups you can make for each set, and complete the division statement.

1. ☒ ☒ ☒ ☒ ☒
   ☒ ☒ ☒ ☒ ☒ _____ groups of 2 **or** 10 ÷ 2 = _____

2. ★ ★ ★ ★ ★
   ★ ★ ★ ★ ★
   ★ ★ ★ ★ ★
   ★ ★ ★ ★ ★ _____ groups of 4 **or** 20 ÷ 4 = _____

3. ✔ ✔ ✔ ✔ ✔
   ✔ ✔ ✔ ✔ ✔
   ✔ ✔ ✔ ✔ ✔ _____ groups of 3 **or** 15 ÷ 3 = _____

Darin has 18 fish in a big tank. He wants to divide the fish into bowls.

4. How many bowls will he need if he wants six fish in each one? _____

5. How many bowls will he need if he wants nine fish in each one? _____

6. How many bowls will he need if he wants three fish in each one? _____

7. How many bowls will he need if he wants two fish in each one? _____

Mrs. Smith has 24 students. Solve these division problems for her.

8. She wants to divide the students into three groups for Computer Lab. How many students will be in each group?

   _____ ÷ _____ = _____ **students**

9. She wants to divide the students into 12 groups for Math. How many students will be in each group?

   _____ ÷ _____ = _____ **students**

10. She wants to divide the students into four groups for Science Lab. How many students will be in each group?

   _____ ÷ _____ = _____ **students**

Started:	Finished:	Total Time:	Completed:	Correct:

Name _____ Date _____

Answer the following questions.

1. How many 3s are in 21? _____

2. How many 10s are in 100? _____

3. How many 9s are in 81? _____

Use the models to solve the division questions.

4. ★ ★ ★ ★ ★
 ★ ★ ★ ★ ★
 ★ ★ ★ ★ ★
 ★ ★ ★ ★ ★

20 ÷ 5 = _____

5.

30 ÷ 3 = _____

6. ▲ ▲ ▲ ▲ ▲ ▲
 ▲ ▲ ▲ ▲ ▲ ▲
 ▲ ▲ ▲ ▲ ▲ ▲
 ▲ ▲ ▲ ▲ ▲ ▲

24 ÷ 4 = _____

Solve the division problems.

7. 8 ÷ 4 = _____   **8.** 28 ÷ 4 = _____

9. 35 ÷ 5 = _____   **10.** 42 ÷ 7 = _____

Started:	Finished:	Total Time:	Completed:	Correct:

Name _____ Date _____

Create two division number sentences for each multiplication number sentence.

1. $2 \times 4 = 8$

_____ ÷ _____ = _____ | _____ ÷ _____ = _____

2. $2 \times 7 = 14$

_____ ÷ _____ = _____ | _____ ÷ _____ = _____

3. $3 \times 4 = 12$

_____ ÷ _____ = _____ | _____ ÷ _____ = _____

Solve the division problems.

4. $9 \div 3 =$ _____

5. $16 \div 8 =$ _____

6. $18 \div 9 =$ _____

7. $30 \div 6 =$ _____

Fill in the blanks to complete the division problems.

8. $25 \div$ _____ $= 5$

9. _____ $\div 6 = 7$

10. $49 \div 7 =$ _____

Started:	Finished:	Total Time:	Completed:	Correct:

Name _____ Date _____

Create two division number sentences for each multiplication number sentence.

1. $3 \times 2 = 6$

_____ ÷ _____ = _____ | _____ ÷ _____ = _____

2. $3 \times 6 = 18$

_____ ÷ _____ = _____ | _____ ÷ _____ = _____

3. $4 \times 6 = 24$

_____ ÷ _____ = _____ | _____ ÷ _____ = _____

4. $4 \times 8 = 32$

_____ ÷ _____ = _____ | _____ ÷ _____ = _____

Fill in the blanks to complete the division problems.

5. $100 \div$ _____ $= 10$ **6.** $56 \div$ _____ $= 8$

Jenna made 36 cupcakes.

7. If she has 6 plates, how many cupcakes should she put on each plate?

$36 \div 6 =$ _____ **cupcakes**

8. If she has 9 plates, how many cupcakes should she put on each plate?

$36 \div 9 =$ _____ **cupcakes**

9. If she has 12 plates, how many cupcakes should she put on each plate?

$36 \div 12 =$ _____ **cupcakes**

10. If she has 4 plates, how many cupcakes should she put on each plate?

$36 \div 4 =$ _____ **cupcakes**

Started:	Finished:	Total Time:	Completed:	Correct:

Name _____ Date _____

Use the models to solve the division questions.

1.

$28 \div 7 =$ _____

2.

$30 \div 10 =$ _____

3.

$42 \div 7 =$ _____

Solve the division problems.

4. $14 \div 7 =$ _____

5. $27 \div 9 =$ _____

6. $32 \div 8 =$ _____

Answer the questions.

7. How many 4s are in 12? _____

8. How many 6s are in 18? _____

9. How many 8s are in 64? _____

10. How many 10s are in 70? _____

Started:	Finished:	Total Time:	Completed:	Correct:

Name _____   Date _____

Solve the division problems.

    1. $24 \div 4 =$ _____

    2. $15 \div 3 =$ _____

    3. $56 \div 8 =$ _____

    4. $63 \div 7 =$ _____

Fill in the blanks to complete the division problems.

    5. _____ $\div 7 = 5$

    6. $48 \div 8 =$ _____

    7. $36 \div$ _____ $= 6$

Use the multiplication number sentences to create two division number sentences.

    8. $5 \times 3 = 15$

    _____ $\div$ _____ $=$ _____ | _____ $\div$ _____ $=$ _____

    9. $4 \times 7 = 28$

    _____ $\div$ _____ $=$ _____ | _____ $\div$ _____ $=$ _____

    10. $5 \times 6 = 30$

    _____ $\div$ _____ $=$ _____ | _____ $\div$ _____ $=$ _____

Started:	Finished:	Total Time:	Completed:	Correct:

Name _____ Date _____

Fill in the blanks to complete the division problems.

1. $24 \div$ _____ $= 4$

2. _____ $\div 3 = 4$

3. $40 \div 10 =$ _____

4. $32 \div$ _____ $= 4$

Solve the division problems.

5. $6 \div 2 =$ _____

6. $9 \div 3 =$ _____

7. $16 \div 4 =$ _____

Show your work. How many groups of ….

8. 4 snakes can be made from 16 snakes?

_____ **groups**

9. 8 turtles can be made from 32 turtles?

_____ **groups**

10. 9 lizards can be made from 45 lizards?

_____ **groups**

Started:	Finished:	Total Time:	Completed:	Correct:

Name _____ Date _____

Answer the questions.

1. How many 2s are in 6? _____

2. How many 5s are in 40? _____

3. How many 7s are in 63? _____

4. How many 3s are in 27? _____

Fill in the blanks to complete the division problems.

5. _____ $\div\ 2 = 10$

6. $72 \div 8 =$ _____

7. $12 \div$ _____ $= 2$

8. $27 \div$ _____ $= 3$

Use the models to solve the division questions.

9. ★ ★ ★ ★ ★
★ ★ ★ ★ ★
★ ★ ★ ★ ★
★ ★ ★ ★ ★
★ ★ ★ ★ ★
★ ★ ★ ★ ★
★ ★ ★ ★ ★
★ ★ ★ ★ ★

$40 \div 8 =$ _____

10.

$63 \div 9 =$ _____

Started:	Finished:	Total Time:	Completed:	Correct:

Name _____   Date _____

Solve the division problems.

1. 32 ÷ 8 = _____   **2.** 24 ÷ 8 = _____

3. 16 ÷ 8 = _____   **4.** 40 ÷ 8 = _____

Answer the questions.

5. How many 3s are in 24? _____

6. How many 5s are in 20? _____

7. How many 6s are in 42? _____

Solve the word problems. Show your work.

8.	Bob had 48 red chairs to set up. He wanted to make 12 rows. How many red chairs would be in each row?
	_____ **chairs**
9.	Nancy cooked 54 large meatballs. She divided them evenly into nine containers. How many meatballs did she put in each container?
	_____ **meatballs**
10.	There are 56 students in the computer lab and 8 computers. If they are divided equally, how many students will share each computer?
	_____ **students**

Started:	Finished:	Total Time:	Completed:	Correct:

Division

Name _____ Date _____

Fill in the blanks to complete the division problems.

1. $15 \div 3 =$ _____

2. _____ $\div 6 = 6$

3. $48 \div 6 =$ _____

4. $20 \div$ _____ $= 5$

Solve the division problems.

5. $21 \div 7 =$ _____

6. $28 \div 7 =$ _____

7. $49 \div 7 =$ _____

8. $56 \div 7 =$ _____

Use the models to complete the division problems.

9.

✔ ✔ ✔ ✔ ✔ ✔ ✔ ✔
✔ ✔ ✔ ✔ ✔ ✔ ✔ ✔
✔ ✔ ✔ ✔ ✔ ✔ ✔ ✔
✔ ✔ ✔ ✔ ✔ ✔ ✔ ✔
✔ ✔ ✔ ✔ ✔ ✔ ✔ ✔

_____ $\div 8 =$ _____

10.

◆ ◆ ◆ ◆ ◆ ◆ ◆ ◆ ◆ ◆ ◆
◆ ◆ ◆ ◆ ◆ ◆ ◆ ◆ ◆ ◆ ◆
◆ ◆ ◆ ◆ ◆ ◆ ◆ ◆ ◆ ◆ ◆

_____ $\div$ _____ $= 11$

Started:	Finished:	Total Time:	Completed:	Correct:

Name _____ Date _____

Solve the division problems.

1. $27 \div 9 =$ _____

2. $54 \div 9 =$ _____

Fill in the blanks to complete the division problems.

3. $45 \div$ _____ $= 5$

4. _____ $\div 9 = 4$

Sam has 12 pretzels. He divided them evenly into cups.

5. How many pretzels did he put in 3 cups? _____ **pretzels**

6. How many pretzels did he put in 6 cups? _____ **pretzels**

7. How many pretzels did he put in 4 cups? _____ **pretzels**

Answer the questions. Show your work.

8. How many 4s are in 16? _____

9. How many 6s are in 30? _____

10. How many 7s are in 35? _____

Started:	Finished:	Total Time:	Completed:	Correct:

Name _____   Date _____

Solve the division problems.

1. $45 \div 5 =$ _____   **2.** $54 \div 6 =$ _____

3. $40 \div 4 =$ _____   **4.** $48 \div 6 =$ _____

Solve the word problems. Show your work.

5. Tia wants to divide her 20 pencils into groups of four. How many groups of pencils can she make?

_____ **groups**

6. Jaden has 36 tennis balls and six buckets. He wants to put the same number of balls in each bucket. How many balls will go in each bucket?

_____ **balls**

7. There are nine boys on the soccer team. Max brought 18 snack bars. How many bars does each player get if the bars are divided evenly?

_____ **bars**

Fill in the blanks to complete the division problems.

8. $81 \div 9 =$ _____   **9.** $63 \div$ _____ $= 7$ **10.** _____ $\div 5 = 9$

Started:	Finished:	Total Time:	Completed:	Correct:

Name _____ Date _____

Solve the word problems. Show your work.

1. How many 5¢ stamps can you buy for 40¢?

_____ **stamps**

2. How many 10¢ stamps can you buy for $1.00?

_____ **stamps**

Answer the questions.

3. How many groups of 3 golf balls can be made if there are 18 golf balls?

_____ **groups of golf balls**

4. How many groups of 3 golf balls can be made if there are 21 golf balls?

_____ **groups of golf balls**

Fill in the blanks to complete the division problems.

5. $60 \div$ _____ $= 12$ **6.** $27 \div$ _____ $= 9$ **7.** $42 \div 6 =$ _____

Use division to complete each task.

8.	Share 21 candies between 7 children. **Each child will receive _____ candies.**
9.	Divide 12 kittens into 4 baskets. **Each basket will have _____ kittens.**
10.	Share 25 books among 5 students. **Each student will get _____ books.**

Started:	Finished:	Total Time:	Completed:	Correct:

Name _____ Date _____

Solve the word problems. Show your work.

1.	Danielle has 24 doll dresses and three dolls. How many dresses does each doll get if the dresses are divided evenly?

_____ **dresses**

2.	Danny has 54 baseball cards. Each page in his scrapbook has 9 spaces. How many pages does he need to store all his cards?

_____ **pages**

Fill in the blanks to complete the division problems.

3. $48 \div$ _____ $= 12$ **4.** $18 \div 6 =$ _____

5. _____ $\div 7 = 5$ **6.** $28 \div$ _____ $= 4$

Look at the group of stars and answer the questions.

★ ★ ★ ★ ★ ★ ★ ★ ★ ★
★ ★ ★ ★ ★ ★ ★ ★ ★ ★
★ ★ ★ ★ ★ ★ ★ ★ ★ ★
★ ★ ★ ★ ★ ★ ★ ★ ★ ★

7. How many stars are there in the group? _____ × _____ = _____

8. How many groups of 10 can you make? _____

9. How many groups of 9 can you make? _____ *remainder* _____

10. How many groups of 7 can you make? _____ *remainder* _____

Started:	Finished:	Total Time:	Completed:	Correct:	

Name _____ Date _____

Use each group of triangles to help you answer the following questions.

1. How many groups of 6 can you make? _____

▲ ▲ ▲ ▲ ▲ ▲
▲ ▲ ▲ ▲ ▲ ▲
▲ ▲ ▲ ▲ ▲ ▲

2. How many groups of 9 can you make? _____

▲ ▲ ▲ ▲ ▲ ▲
▲ ▲ ▲ ▲ ▲ ▲
▲ ▲ ▲ ▲ ▲ ▲

3. How many groups of 4 can you make? _____ *remainder* _____

▲ ▲ ▲ ▲ ▲ ▲ ▲ ▲
▲ ▲ ▲ ▲ ▲ ▲ ▲ ▲

4. How many groups of 7 can you make? _____ *remainder* _____

▲ ▲ ▲ ▲ ▲ ▲ ▲ ▲
▲ ▲ ▲ ▲ ▲ ▲ ▲ ▲

Solve the division problems.

5. $51 \div 10 =$ _____ *remainder* _____   **6.** $47 \div 8 =$ _____ *remainder* _____

7. $39 \div 6 =$ _____ *remainder* _____   **8.** $27 \div 5 =$ _____ *remainder* _____

Solve these word problems with remainders. Show your work.

9.	There were 28 pencils in the bucket for 6 students. How many pencils did each student get? _____ How many pencils were left over? _____
10.	If you shared 20 erasers among 6 children, how many erasers would each child get? _____ How many erasers would be left over? _____

Started:	Finished:	Total Time:	Completed:	Correct:

Name _____ Date _____

Complete each division problem.

1. $9 \div 4 =$ _____ *remainder* _____

2. $20 \div 7 =$ _____ *remainder* _____

3. $18 \div 4 =$ _____ *remainder* _____

4. $22 \div 7 =$ _____ *remainder* _____

There are 15 ants and they all must go into ant houses.

5. If four ants can go in each ant house, how many ant houses do you need?

$15 \div 4 =$ _____ *remainder* _____   _____ **houses**

6. How many ant houses will have four ants? _____

7. How many ants will be in the last house? _____

A teacher wants to divide 17 toy animals evenly among 5 children.

8. Write the division problem to solve the teachers' problem.

_____ $\div$ _____ = _____ *remainder* _____

9. How many toy animals will each child get? _____

10. How many toy animals will be left over? _____

Started:	Finished:	Total Time:	Completed:	Correct:

Name _____ Date _____

Solve the problems.

1.   24
      + 56
    _____

2.   98
      − 37
    _____

3. $8 \times 7 =$ _____

4. $36 \div 9 =$ _____

Use multiplication to check that you have divided correctly.

5. $30 \div 6 =$ _____ $6 \times$ _____ $= 30$

6. $54 \div 9 =$ _____ $9 \times$ _____ $= 54$

7. $77 \div 7 =$ _____ $7 \times$ _____ $= 77$

8. $24 \div 4 =$ _____ $4 \times$ _____ $= 24$

Solve the problems. Circle the operation you used and show your work.

9.	Saul built 5 fences every week for 4 weeks.
	How many fences did Saul build? _____
	Addition Subtraction Multiplication Division
10.	Daniel built 16 fences in four weeks. He built the same number of fences each week.
	How many fences did he build each week? _____
	Addition Subtraction Multiplication Division

Started:	Finished:	Total Time:	Completed:	Correct:

Name _____ Date _____

Solve the problems.

1. 23
    + 43

2. 99
    − 34

3. 17
    + 18

4. 67
    − 23

5. 10 + 10 + 10 + 10 + 10 + 10 = _____

6. 50
    − 46

7. 40 ÷ 8 = _____

8. 3 × 9 = _____

Solve the problems. Circle the operation you used and show your work.

9.	Terry made 21 cookies for the party. Marla made 12 cookies, and Mom made 38 cookies. How many cookies did they have for the party?

_____ cookies

Addition   Subtraction   Multiplication   Division

10.	The birthday cake was cut and put on plates. There were three rows of plates. Each row had five plates of cake. How many pieces of cake were there altogether?

_____ pieces of cake

Addition   Subtraction   Multiplication   Division

Started:	Finished:	Total Time:	Completed:	Correct:

Name _____ Date _____

Solve each problem. Watch out for remainders.

1. $26 \div 6 =$ _____ *remainder* _____

2. $14 \div 3 =$ _____ *remainder* _____

3. $23 \div 5 =$ _____ *remainder* _____

Multiply to solve.

4. $8 \times 4 =$ _____

5. $5 \times 12 =$ _____

6. $7 \times 4 =$ _____

Subtract to solve.

7. $\begin{array}{r} 73 \\ -\ 39 \\ \hline \end{array}$

8. $\begin{array}{r} 100 \\ -\ 54 \\ \hline \end{array}$

Solve the problems. Circle the operation you used and show your work.

9.	Jamie has 13 sweaters. Seven sweaters are too small. How many sweaters does she have that still fit?
	Addition Subtraction Multiplication Division
10.	There are five children and each child has three pairs of shoes. How many pairs of shoes do the children have altogether?
	Addition Subtraction Multiplication Division

Started:	Finished:	Total Time:	Completed:	Correct:

Name _____   Date _____

Solve the problems.

1. $7 + 5 =$ _____   **2.** $7 \times 5 =$ _____

3. $7 - 5 =$ _____   **4.** $7 \div 5 =$ _____ remainder _____

Place the correct sign (+, –, ×, or ÷) in each number sentence.

5. $72 \bigcirc 8 = 9$ **6.** $7 \bigcirc 6 = 42$

Solve the problems.

7.   89
    + 15

8.   53
    – 24

Solve the problems. Circle the operation you used and show your work.

9.	A giant pizza was cut into 20 slices. If 10 people were going to share the pizza, how many slices would each person get?
	Addition **Subtraction** **Multiplication** **Division**
10.	Tracy found a box with 25 stuffed animals. She chose eight animals. How many stuffed animals did Tracy leave in the box?
	Addition **Subtraction** **Multiplication** **Division**

Started:	Finished:	Total Time:	Completed:	Correct:

Name _____   Date _____

What is the value of each group of coins? Show your work.

1.   6 quarters _____ × _____ = _____

2.   8 pennies _____ × _____ = _____

3.   6 nickels _____ × _____ = _____

4.   9 dimes _____ × _____ = _____

If one raffle ticket costs a dime, how much will …

5. 8 tickets cost? _____

6. 10 tickets cost? _____

7. 20 tickets cost? _____

8. 4 tickets cost? _____

Solve the problems. Show your work.

9.	Three sisters each paid $4.00 to go to the movies. How much did the tickets cost altogether?
10.	There are eight students in the math club. They have each saved the same amount of money. If they have $80 altogether, how much money has each student saved?

Started:	Finished:	Total Time:	Completed:	Correct:

Name _____   Date _____

If one ball costs \$3.00 how much will …

1. 3 balls cost? _____ × _____ = \$_____

2. 8 balls cost? _____ × _____ = \$_____

3. 5 balls cost? _____ × _____ = \$_____

Add the money in each group to find the total.

4. 🪙🪙🪙🪙🪙 + 🪙🪙 + 🪙🪙 = _____

5. 🪙🪙 + 🪙🪙🪙🪙 + 🪙🪙 = _____

6. 🪙🪙🪙 + 🪙🪙🪙🪙 🪙🪙🪙 + 🪙🪙🪙🪙🪙 = _____

Look at the menu to find out what each student will spend for lunch.

School Lunch Menu	
Taco	\$2.00
Pizza	\$3.50
Hot Dog	\$2.50
Salad	\$1.50
Soup	\$1.75

7. Jim ordered a taco and soup. He spent _____ + _____ = _____

8. Chris chose pizza and a salad. He spent _____ + _____ = _____

9. Rob chose a taco and a salad. He spent _____ + _____ = _____

10. Michael ordered soup and salad. He spent _____ + _____ = _____

Started:	Finished:	Total Time:	Completed:	Correct:

Name _____ Date _____

If one pencil costs 9¢, how much will ...

1. 6 pencils cost? _____ × _____ = _____ ¢

2. 4 pencils cost? _____ × _____ = _____ ¢

3. 9 pencils cost? _____ × _____ = _____ ¢

Use the price list to see how much money each student spent.

Binder	**$3.25**
Notebook	**$2.50**
Lunch Box	**$4.75**
Ruler	**$0.75**
Pencil	**$0.50**

4. Randi bought a binder and notebook. _____ + _____ = _____

5. Teri got a lunch box and 2 pencils. _____ + _____ + _____ = _____

6. Lauri needed 2 binders and 1 ruler. _____ + _____ + _____ = _____

7. Kristi bought a notebook and a ruler. _____ + _____ = _____

How much money does each student have?

8. Jack has and _____

9. Jill has and  and  _____

10. Thom has  and  _____

Started:	Finished:	Total Time:	Completed:	Correct:

Name _____ Date _____

Show your work. If one drink costs 50¢ how much will …

1. 4 drinks cost? _____

2. 6 drinks cost? _____

3. 8 drinks cost? _____

4. 10 drinks cost? _____

5. 3 drinks cost? _____

Add to find how much each student spent on tickets at the fair.

6.	Mila spent $55 on tickets for her cousin and $55 on tickets for herself.
7.	Jonas spent $102 on tickets in the morning and $39 on tickets in the afternoon.

Which option is more money? Circle your choice.

8. (5 quarters)   **or**   ($1 bill)

9. (7 dimes)   **or**   (14 nickels)

10. (3 dimes)   **or**   (32 pennies)

Started:	Finished:	Total Time:	Completed:	Correct:

Name _____   Date _____

Write the fraction that names the shaded portion in each shape.

1. _____

2. _____

3. _____

> two thirds
>
> one half
>
> one quarter

Shade the shapes to show the fractions.

4.  $\frac{2}{4}$ 5. 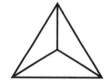 $\frac{1}{3}$ 6. $\frac{3}{4}$

Look at the circled part of each collection. Fill in the blank to show what part of the fraction it is.

7.  = $\frac{}{4}$

8.  = $\frac{}{8}$

9.  = $\frac{}{6}$

10.   = $\frac{}{8}$

Started:	Finished:	Total Time:	Completed:	Correct:

Name _____ Date _____

Fill in the blank and circle the given part of each group of balls.

1. $\frac{2}{8}$ of 8 tennis balls = _____ tennis balls

2. $\frac{3}{4}$ of 4 soccer balls = _____ soccer balls

3. $\frac{2}{6}$ of 6 footballs = _____ footballs

Write the fraction that names the shaded portion in each shape.

4. 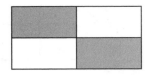 _____

5. 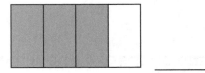 _____

6. 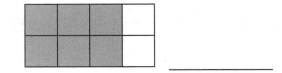 _____

7. _____

Place >, <, or = between the two fraction circles to complete each statement.

8.

9.

10.

Started:	Finished:	Total Time:	Completed:	Correct:

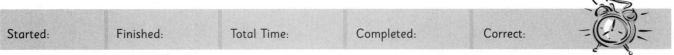

Name _____ Date _____

Write a fraction to show the circled part of each group.

1. (🍎 🍎 🍎) 🍎 = $\frac{}{4}$

2. 🍊 (🍊) = $\frac{}{2}$

3. (🍐 🍐 🍐) 🍐 🍐 🍐 = $\frac{}{6}$

4. 🍌 🍌 (🍌 🍌 🍌 🍌 🍌 🍌) = $\frac{}{8}$

Circle the fraction that is greater.

5.	6.	7.
$\frac{1}{4}$ or $\frac{2}{4}$	$\frac{6}{6}$ or $\frac{5}{6}$	$\frac{2}{3}$ or $\frac{1}{3}$

Write the fraction that names the shaded portion in each shape.

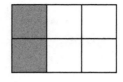

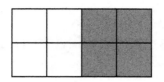

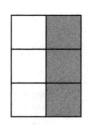

8. _____

9. _____

10. _____

Started:	Finished:	Total Time:	Completed:	Correct:

Name _____   Date _____

Shade the fraction indicated on each shape.

1. $\frac{1}{3}$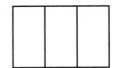

2. $\frac{3}{4}$

3. $\frac{1}{2}$

Compare each pair of fractions. Circle the fraction that is less.

| 4. | $\frac{1}{3}$ | 5. | $\frac{2}{3}$ | 6. | $\frac{5}{8}$ |
| | $\frac{1}{4}$ | | $\frac{2}{8}$ | | $\frac{3}{4}$ |

Order the set of fractions from *least* to *greatest*.

7. $\frac{7}{8}$, $\frac{2}{8}$, $\frac{1}{8}$, $\frac{8}{8}$ → _____ _____ _____ _____

Circle $\frac{3}{8}$ of the ladybugs.

8.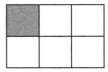

Write the fraction that names the shaded portion in each shape.

9.  _____

10. _____

Started: Finished: Total Time: Completed: Correct:

Name _____   Date _____

Write the correct letter to match each fraction.

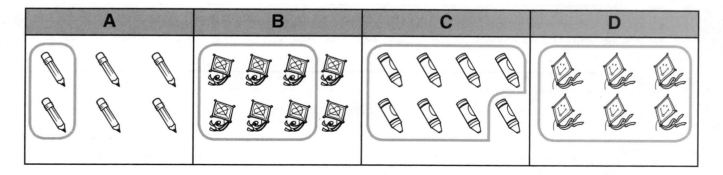

A	B	C	D

1. $\frac{6}{6}$ _____   2. $\frac{7}{8}$ _____   3. $\frac{6}{8}$ or $\frac{3}{4}$ _____   4. $\frac{2}{6}$ or $\frac{1}{3}$ _____

Write a fraction to describe each set of shaded shamrocks.

5. [shamrocks] $= \dfrac{}{8}$ 6. [shamrocks] $= \dfrac{}{8}$

Shade the two fractions in each row. Then, use the correct sign (<, >, or =) to compare them.

7. [   ] $\frac{1}{4}$  $\frac{2}{8}$ [   ]

8. [   ] $\frac{5}{6}$ ◯ $\frac{3}{6}$ [   ]

9. [   ] $\frac{8}{8}$ ◯ $\frac{3}{4}$ [   ]

10. [   ] $\frac{2}{3}$ ◯ $\frac{4}{6}$ [   ]

Started:	Finished:	Total Time:	Completed:	Correct:

Name _____ Date _____

Show each fraction on the number lines.

1. $\frac{4}{8}$ 0 |___|___|___|___|___|___|___|___| 1

2. $\frac{2}{8}$ 0 |___|___|___|___|___|___|___|___| 1

3. $\frac{6}{8}$ 0 |___|___|___|___|___|___|___|___| 1

4. $\frac{3}{6}$ 0 |___|___|___|___|___|___| 1

5. $\frac{6}{6}$ 0 |___|___|___|___|___|___| 1

Add or subtract the fractions.

6. $\frac{1}{3} + \frac{1}{3} = \ \overline{3}$

7. $\frac{3}{4} - \frac{1}{4} = \ \overline{4}$

8. $\frac{1}{6} + \frac{2}{6} + \frac{1}{6} = \ \overline{6}$

9. $\frac{2}{3} - \frac{1}{3} = \ \overline{3}$

10. $\frac{2}{8} + \frac{2}{8} + \frac{1}{8} = \ \overline{8}$

Started:	Finished:	Total Time:	Completed:	Correct:

Name _____   Date _____

Circle the time shown on each of the clocks.

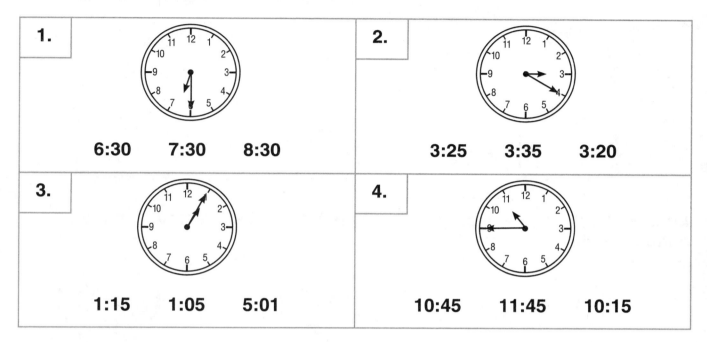

1.

6:30   7:30   8:30

2.

3:25   3:35   3:20

3.

1:15   1:05   5:01

4.

10:45   11:45   10:15

Circle *true* or *false* to answer each of the statements.

5. A *quarter after three* and *three fifteen* are the same time. **true   false**

6. *Six forty-five* and a *quarter to seven* are the same time. **true   false**

7. *Half past nine* and *nine fifteen* are the same time. **true   false**

8. *Half past six* and *six thirty* are the same time. **true   false**

Write the time shown on each analog clock.

9.

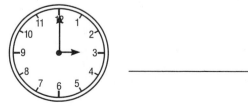

_____

10.

_____

Started:	Finished:	Total Time:	Completed:	Correct:

Name _____ Date _____

Look at the analog clocks. Write the same time on the digital clocks.

1.
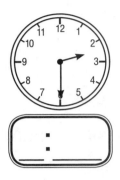

2.
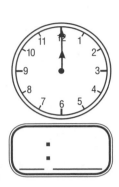

3.
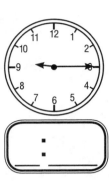

Look at the digital clocks. Draw the hands for the same times on the analog clocks.

4.

5.

6.

Write the time shown on each of the analog clocks.

7.
 _____

8.
 _____

9.
 _____

10.
 _____

Started:	Finished:	Total Time:	Completed:	Correct:

Name _____ Date _____

Match the time shown on each of the clocks to the correct words.

A. 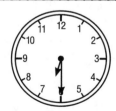 **B.**  **C.**  **D.**

1. quarter to eight _____   **2.** noon _____

3. half past six _____   **4.** quarter after four _____

Look at each analog clock. What time will it be in 30 minutes?

5.    **6.**    **7.**    **8.**

_____   _____   _____   _____

Solve the word problems.

9.	It is 4 o'clock. Tripp has soccer practice in one hour. What time does Tripp have to be at practice? ____:____
10.	Mimi has a two-hour skating lesson. It starts at 1:30. What time does her practice end? ____:____

Name _____ Date _____

Look at the analog clocks. Write the same time on the digital clocks.

1.

2.

3.

Look at the digital clocks. Draw the hands on the analog clocks to match.

4.

```
10:25
```

5.

```
3:55
```

6.

```
12:35
```

Write the time shown on each of the analog clocks.

7.

8.

9.

10.
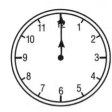

_____   _____   _____   _____

Started:	Finished:	Total Time:	Completed:	Correct:

Name _____   Date _____

What time will it be if you add 15 minutes to each time?

1. 12:00 + 15 minutes = _____ : _____

2. 3:15 + 15 minutes = _____ : _____

3. 4:30 + 15 minutes = _____ : _____

4. 9:45 + 15 minutes = _____ : _____

Circle *true* or *false* to answer each of the statements.

5. A quarter after nine and **nine forty-five** are the same time.   **true**   **false**

6. Seven forty-five and **a quarter to eight** are the same time.   **true**   **false**

7. Half past noon and **twelve-thirty** are the same time.   **true**   **false**

8. Two forty-five and **three fifteen** are the same time.   **true**   **false**

What time will it be if you add 30 minutes to each time?

9. 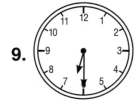   6:30 + 30 minutes = _____ : _____

10. 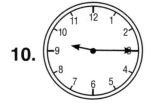   9:15 + 30 minutes = _____ : _____

Started:	Finished:	Total Time:	Completed:	Correct:

Name _____ Date _____

Read each word problem. Answer each question about time.

1.	Joe started his homework at 2 o'clock. He finished at 4:30. How long did Joe work?

_____

2.	Shelby started her project at 1:45 and finished 8 hours later. At what time did she finish her project?

3.	Sara finished her painting at 7 pm. She painted for three hours. What time did she start her painting?

What time will it be if you add ten minutes to each time?

4. 4:20 + 10 minutes   **5.** 1:10 + 10 minutes   **6.** 3:20 + 10 minutes

_____ **:** _____   _____ **:** _____   _____ **:** _____

Write the time shown on each of the analog clocks on the lines below.

7. _____   **8.** _____   **9.** _____   **10.** _____

Started:	Finished:	Total Time:	Completed:	Correct:

Name _____ Date _____

Circle the name of the shape at the beginning of each row.

1.   square   triangle   rhombus   oval

2.   square   circle   triangle   oval

3.   circle   triangle   rhombus   oval

4.   square   circle   triangle   oval

Look at the first figure in the row. Circle its match in the row.

5. |

6. |

7.

Circle the letter for the shape in each row that is *not* a quadrilateral.

8.

    A   B   C   D

9.

    A   B   C   D

Circle the letter for the shape that is *not* an octagon.

10.

    A   B   C   D

Started:	Finished:	Total Time:	Completed:	Correct:

Name _____ Date _____

Fill in each blank with the correct answer.

1. A square has _____ corners.

2. A triangle has _____ corners.

3. A circle has _____ corners.

4. A pentagon has _____ corners.

Look at each shape and count the sides.

5. A rhombus has _____ sides.

6. An octagon has _____ sides.

7. A hexagon has _____ sides.

Look at the first shape. Circle the next shape in each row that is congruent. *Congruent* **means having exactly the same size and shape.**

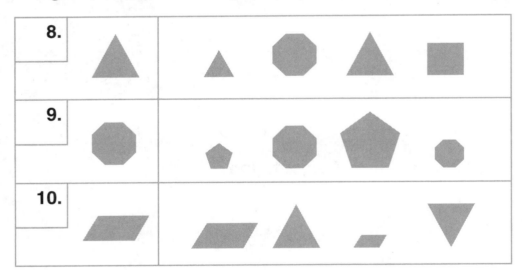

Started: Finished: Total Time: Completed: Correct:

Name _____ Date _____

Find the perimeter of each shape.

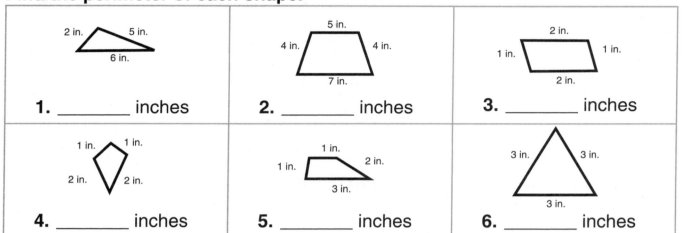

1. _____ inches	2. _____ inches	3. _____ inches
4. _____ inches	5. _____ inches	6. _____ inches

Solve the word problems. Add measurements to the shapes to help you.

7. One side of a square is 4 inches. What is the perimeter of the square?

_____ **inches**

8. The two short sides of the rectangle are 2 inches long.
The two long sides of the rectangle are each 6 inches long.

What is the perimeter of the rectangle? _____ **inches**

Circle *true* or *false* to answer each of the statements.

9. All four sides of a rectangle are the same length.   **true**   **false**

10. To find the perimeter of a shape, add all the sides.   **true**   **false**

Started:	Finished:	Total Time:	Completed:	Correct:

Name _____ Date _____

Find the perimeter of each quadrilateral.

1.
6"
3" | | 3"
6"

2.
4"
2" / \ 2"
6"

3.
5"
5" | | 5"
5"

perimeter _____ perimeter _____ perimeter _____

Circle *true* or *false* to answer each of the statements.

4.
2"
2" | | 2"
2"
The perimeter of this shape is 8 inches.   **true**   **false**

5.
3 yds. /\ 3 yds.
3 yds.
The perimeter of this shape is 9 yards.   **true**   **false**

6.
4 ft.
2 ft. | | 2 ft.
4 ft.
The perimeter of this shape is 10 feet.   **true**   **false**

The perimeter of each shape is 20 cm. Find the length of the missing side.

7.
8 cm
? cm ____/ 3 cm
6 cm

8.
4 cm ? cm
6 cm \/ 6 cm

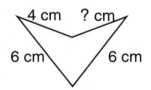

Solve the word problems.

9. The garden is 20 feet long and 10 feet wide. What is the perimeter?

_____

10. The beach towel is 4 feet long and 2 feet wide. What is the perimeter?

_____

Started:	Finished:	Total Time:	Completed:	Correct:

Name _____   Date _____

Circle the name of each solid shape.

1.   cone   sphere   cube   prism   cylinder

2.   cone   sphere   cube   prism   cylinder

3.   cone   sphere   cube   prism   cylinder

4.   cone   sphere   cube   prism   cylinder

5.   cone   sphere   cube   prism   cylinder

Which shape below is not a solid shape? Circle your answer.

6.

    A.   **B.**   **C.**   **D.**

Match each solid shape to an item in the box. Write the letter for each answer.

7. cylinder _____

8. cube _____

9. sphere _____

10. rectangular prism _____

 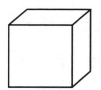 

A.   **B.**

C.   **D.**

Started:	Finished:	Total Time:	Completed:	Correct:

Name _____ Date _____

Circle the name of each solid shape.

1.   triangular prism   cone   sphere

2.   cube   rectangular prism   cone

3.   cylinder   sphere   cone   cube

4.   cylinder   cube   triangular prism

How many faces does each solid shape have?

5.   _____ faces

6. 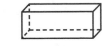   _____ faces

7.    _____ faces

Look at the faces on each solid shape. What two shapes are used?

8.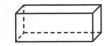

_____   _____

9.

_____   _____

How many corners does a cube have?

10. A cube has _____ corners.

Started:	Finished:	Total Time:	Completed:	Correct:

Name _____ Date _____

Circle the best measurement to find the area of the following items.

1. TV screen   **inches²**   or   **yards²**

2. tennis court   **inches²**   or   **yards²**

3. classroom floor   **inches²**   or   **yards²**

4. box of crayons   **inches²**   or   **yards²**

Use the grids to find the area of the gray squares. Each square equals 1 square foot.

5.

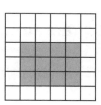

The area is _____ square feet.

6.

The area is _____ square feet.

If the area of this shape **is 3 units², what is the area of each of the shapes below?**

7. _____ units²

8. _____ units²

9. _____ units²

10. _____ units²

Started:	Finished:	Total Time:	Completed:	Correct:

Name _____ Date _____

Find the area of each quadrilateral.

1.

2.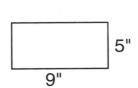

3.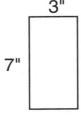

Area = _____ sq. in. | Area = _____ sq. in. | Area = _____ sq. in.

Compare the two rectangles.

Rectangle A

Rectangle B

4. What is the area of *Rectangle A*? _____ **square units**

5. Is the area of *Rectangle A* the same as the area of *Rectangle B*? **yes   no**

Find the area of the white part of each shape. Show the area in units.

6.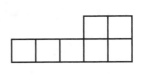

7.

8.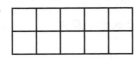

_____ units² | _____ units² | _____ units²

Chose the best measurement to find the area of the following items.

9. placemat   **inches²**   or   **yards²**

10. basketball court   **inches²**   or   **yards²**

| Started: | Finished: | Total Time: | Completed: | Correct: |

Name _____   Date _____

Answer the questions below. Write the letter for each answer.

A.  **B.**  **C.**  **D.**

1. Which measuring cup shows $\frac{1}{2}$ cup? _____

2. Which measuring cup shows $\frac{3}{4}$ cup? _____

3. Which measuring cup shows $\frac{1}{4}$ cup? _____

If there are two pints in one quart, how many pints are in

4. 3 quarts? _____   **5.** 5 quarts? _____

If there are four quarts in one gallon, how many quarts are in

6. 2 gallons? _____   **7.** 4 gallons? _____

Use the pictures to answer the questions below.

 teaspoon   pool   teacup    bucket

8. Which item will hold more than two gallons of water? _____

9. Which item will hold the least amount of water? _____

10. Which item would be best to hold one gallon of water? _____

Started:	Finished:	Total Time:	Completed:	Correct:

Name _____ Date _____

Circle the best estimate for each item. Use the samples to help you.

1 gram (1g) =   **1 kilogram (1kg) =**

1. pencil	25 grams	25 kilograms
2. melon	2 grams	2 kilograms
3. penny	2 grams	2 kilograms
4. bottle of water	1 gram	1 kilogram

Answer the questions about the liter containers.

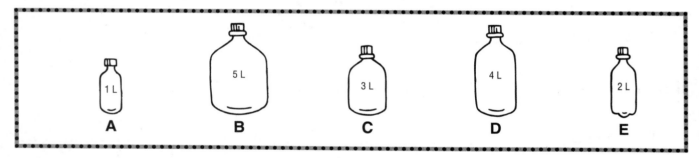

5. If 1 liter = 1,000 milliliters then 2 liters = _____ milliliters

6. Which liter container would hold the least amount of water? _____

7. Which liter container would hold the most water? _____

8. Which liter container is half the size of container **D**? _____

9. Which liter container would hold 5 times more than container **A**? _____

10. Would a bathtub hold more than container **B**? _____

Started:	Finished:	Total Time:	Completed:	Correct:

Name _____ Date _____

Answer the questions.

1. How many inches are in one foot? _____ *inches*

2. How many feet are in one yard? _____ *feet*

3. How many inches are in one yard? _____ *inches*

Convert each measurement from inches to feet.

4. 24 inches equals _____ *feet*

5. 48 inches equals _____ *feet*

6. 60 inches equals _____ *feet*

Convert each measurement from feet to inches.

7. 3 feet equals _____ *inches*

8. 6 feet equals _____ *inches*

Convert each measurement to feet and inches. Show your work.

9. 59 inches equals _____ *feet* and _____ *inches*

10. 28 inches equals _____ *feet* and _____ *inches*

Started:	Finished:	Total Time:	Completed:	Correct:

Name _____   Date _____

One sunflower seed is $\frac{1}{2}$ inch long.

1. How long would 2 sunflower seeds be? _____

2. How long would 3 sunflower seeds be? _____

3. How long would 5 sunflower seeds be? _____

There are 12 inches in one foot.

4. How many inches are there in 2 feet? _____ *inches*

5. How many inches are there in 4 feet? _____ *inches*

6. How many inches are there in 6 feet? _____ *inches*

There are 3 feet in a yard.

7. How many feet are there in 2 yards? _____ *feet*

8. How many feet are there in 10 yards? _____ *feet*

Solve the word problems. Show your work.

9.	Cole found three golden keys. Each one was two inches long.
	How long were they when he lined them up? _____ *inches*
10.	Lauren helped her dad build a new fence. They built six feet of fence each day. They worked for six days.
	How many feet of fence did they build? _____ *feet*

Started:	Finished:	Total Time:	Completed:	Correct:

Name _____   Date _____

Compare the thermometers to answer the questions below.

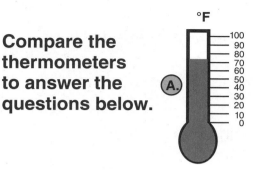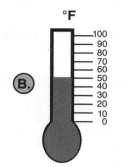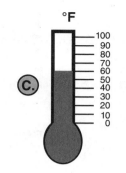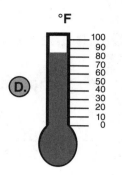

1. Which thermometer shows the hottest temperature? _____

2. What is the hottest temperature shown? _____°F

3. Which thermometer shows the coolest temperature? _____

4. What is the coolest temperature shown? _____°F

Show the temperatures on the thermometers.

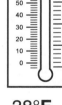

5. 100°F   **6.** 38°F   **7.** -10°C   **8.** 38°C

Solve the word problems.

9. It is 48°F in the mountains and 88° F at the beach.
How much colder is it in the mountains? _____ °F

10. Rylan said that it was only -10°C when she
woke up. By lunch time was 10°C.
How many degrees warmer did it get? _____ °C

Started:	Finished:	Total Time:	Completed:	Correct:

Name _____   Date _____

Circle the best measurement tool for each measurement needed.

1. temperature   measuring cup   thermometer   yardstick

2. height   measuring tape   measuring cup   scale

3. salt for a recipe   measuring cup   yardstick   thermometer

4. weight   scale   yardstick   measuring tape

Choose the unit of measure you would use to measure each item.

inches	ounces	gallons	pounds

5. length of a bed _____

6. weight of a backpack filled with books _____

7. weight of water in a water bottle _____

16 ounces = 1 pound

8. If a watermelon weighs two pounds, how many
ounces does it weigh?   _____ **ounces**

9. Johan has four boxes of trading cards.
Each box weights four ounces. How many
ounces do the four boxes weigh altogether?   _____ **ounces**

10. Which is more — *one pound* or *eight ounces*? _____

Started:	Finished:	Total Time:	Completed:	Correct:

Name _____   Date _____

Use the graph to answer the questions.

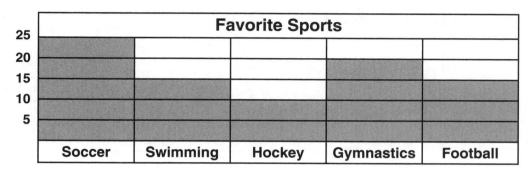

	Favorite Sports			

1. Which sport got the most votes? _____

2. Which sport received the fewest votes? _____

3. What is the difference between the most votes and the fewest votes?

_____

4. Which two sports received the same number of votes?

_____   _____

Use the circle chart to answer the questions.

5. What is the least common way to get to school? _____

6. Which way do most students use to get to school? _____

7. Which two ways had the same amount? _____ _____

Use this chart to answer the questions.

Black	White	Silver	Red
3	9	6	12

8. What was the most common color? _____

9. Which color is counted three times more than black? _____

10. Which color is counted two times more than silver? _____

Name _____ Date _____

Use the circle chart to answer the questions.

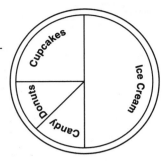

1. Which treat did half of the voters like? _____

2. Which treat did ¼ of the voters like? _____

3. Which two treats got the same number of votes?

_____   _____

Use the Eye Colors chart to answer the questions below.

EYE COLORS	
Green	‖‖
Blue	‖‖ ‖
Hazel	‖‖
Brown	‖‖ ‖‖

4. Most students have _____ eyes.

5. _____ is the color the fewest students have.

6. The difference between the brown and the hazel eyes is

_____.

7. Together, the _____ eyes and the _____ eyes equal 12.

Use the graph to answer the questions.

Number of 1st Place Medals Won										
Jack	▓	▓	▓	▓	▓	▓	▓	▓	▓	
Jeff	▓	▓	▓	▓						
Jill	▓	▓	▓	▓	▓	▓				
Jett	▓	▓	▓	▓	▓	▓	▓	▓	▓	▓
	1	2	3	4	5	6	7	8	9	10

8. How many medals did Jack and Jill win? _____

9. Who won the most medals? _____

10. Who won the fewest medals? _____

Started:	Finished:	Total Time:	Completed:	Correct:

Common Core State Standards Correlation

Pages in *Timed Math Practice* meet one or more of the following Common Core State Standards © Copyright 2010. National Governors Association Center for Best Practices and Council of Chief State School Officers. All rights reserved. For more information about the Common Core State Standards, go to *http://www.corestandards. org/* or *http://www.teachercreated.com/standards/*.

Mathematics Standards	Test
Operations and Algebraic Thinking	
3.OA.1. Interpret products of whole numbers, e.g., interpret 5 x 7 as the total number of objects in 5 groups of 7 objects each. *For example*, describe a context in which a total number of objects can be expressed as 5 x 7.	36–37, 39–42, 45–48, 65–72, 96
3.OA.2. Interpret whole-number quotients of whole numbers, e.g., interpret 56 ÷ 8 as the number of objects in each share when 56 objects are partitioned equally into 8 shares, or as a number of shares when 56 objects are partitioned into equal shares of 8 objects each. *For example, describe a context in which a number of shares or a number of groups can be expressed as 56 ÷ 8.*	49–50, 52–53, 55–65, 68
3.OA.3. Use multiplication and division within 100 to solve word problems in situations involving equal groups, arrays, and measurement quantities, e.g., by using drawings and equations with a symbol for the unknown number to represent a problem.	48–50, 53, 56–58, 60–66, 68–72, 95–96
3.OA.4. Determine the unknown whole number in multiplication or division equations relating three whole numbers. *For example, determine the unknown number that makes the equation true in each of the equations 8 x ? = 48, 5 = ? ÷ 3, 6 x 6 = ?*	38–40, 42–51, 54–69
3.OA.5. Apply properties of operations as strategies to multiply and divide. *Examples: If 6 × 4 = 24 is known, then 4 × 6 = 24 is also known. (Commutative property of multiplication.) 3 × 5 × 2 can be found by 3 × 5 = 15, then 15 × 2 = 30, or by 5 × 2 = 10, then 3 × 10 = 30. (Associative property of multiplication.) Knowing that 8 × 5 = 40 and 8 × 2 = 16, one can find 8 × 7 as 8 × (5 + 2) = (8 × 5) + (8 × 2) = 40 + 16 = 56. (Distributive property.)*	36, 38, 41, 43, 46, 50–52, 54–55, 65
3.OA.6. Understand division as an unknown-factor problem. *For example, find 32 ÷ 8 by finding the number that makes 32 when multiplied by 8.*	50–52, 56, 59–68
3.OA.7. Fluently multiply and divide within 100, using strategies such as the relationship between multiplication and division (e.g., knowing that 8 × 5 = 40, one knows 40 ÷ 5 = 8) or properties of operations. By the end of grade 3, know from memory all products of the two one-digit numbers.	51–52, 55, 58–72
3.OA.8. Solve two-step word problems using the four operations. Represent these problems using equations with a letter standing for the unknown quantity. Assess the reasonableness of answers using mental computation and estimation strategies including rounding.	39–40, 45, 47–48, 52, 55, 57, 59–72, 96
3.OA.9. Identify arithmetic patterns (including patterns in the addition table or multiplication table), and explain them using properties of operations. *For example, observe that 4 times a number is always even, and explain why 4 times a number can be decomposed into two equal addends.*	13
Number and Operations in Base Ten	
3.NBT.1. Use place value understanding to round whole numbers to the nearest 10 or 100.	17
3.NBT.2. Fluently add and subtract within 1000 using strategies and algorithms based on place value, properties of operations, and/or the relationship between addition and subtraction.	8–14, 16, 39, 65–66, 68, 70–72, 97
3.NBT.3. Multiply one-digit whole numbers by multiples of 10 in the range 10–90 (e.g., 9 × 80, 5 × 60) using strategies based on place value and properties of operations.	69, 72, 96
Number and Operations—Fractions	
3.NF.1. Understand a fraction 1/*b* as the quantity formed by 1 part when a whole is partitioned into *b* equal parts; understand a fraction *a/b* as the quantity formed by *a* parts of size 1/*b*.	73–78
3.NF.2. Understand a fraction as a number on the number line; represent fractions on a number line diagram.	78

3.NF.3. Explain equivalence of fractions in special cases, and compare fractions by reasoning about their size.	74–78
a. Understand two fractions as equivalent (equal) if they are the same size, or the same point on a number line.	
b. Recognize and generate simple equivalent fractions, e.g., 1/2 = 2/4, 4/6 = 2/3. Explain why the fractions are equivalent, e.g., by using a visual fraction model.	
d. Compare two fractions with the same numerator or the same denominator by reasoning about their size. Recognize that comparisons are valid only when the two fractions refer to the same whole. Record the results of comparisons with the symbols >, =, or <, and justify the conclusions, e.g., by using a visual fraction model.	
Measurement and Data	
3.MD.1. Tell and write time to the nearest minute and measure time intervals in minutes. Solve word problems involving addition and subtraction of time intervals in minutes, e.g., by representing the problem on a number line diagram.	79–84
3.MD.2. Measure and estimate liquid volumes and masses of objects using standard units of grams (g), kilograms (kg), and liters (l). Add, subtract, multiply, or divide to solve one-step word problems involving masses or volumes that are given in the same units, e.g., by using drawings (such as a beaker with a measurement scale) to represent the problem.	93–94, 98
3.MD.3. Draw a scaled picture graph and a scaled bar graph to represent a data set with several categories. Solve one- and two-step "how many more" and "how many less" problems using information presented in scaled bar graphs. *For example, draw a bar graph in which each square in the bar graph might represent 5 pets.*	99–100
3.MD.5. Recognize area as an attribute of plane figures and understand concepts of area measurement.	91
a. A square with side length 1 unit, called "a unit square," is said to have "one square unit" of area, and can be used to measure area.	
b. A plane figure which can be covered without gaps or overlaps by *n* unit squares is said to have an area of *n* square units.	
3.MD.6. Measure areas by counting unit squares (square cm, square m, square in., square ft., and improvised units).	91–92
3.MD.7. Relate area to the operations of multiplication and addition.	91–92
b. Multiply side lengths to find areas of rectangles with whole-number side lengths in the context of solving real world and mathematical problems, and represent whole-number products as rectangular areas in mathematical reasoning.	
c. Use tiling to show in a concrete case that the area of a rectangle with whole-number side lengths a and $b + c$ is the sum of $a \times b$ and $a \times c$. Use area models to represent the distributive property in mathematical reasoning.	
3.MD.8. Solve real world and mathematical problems involving perimeters of polygons, including finding the perimeter given the side lengths, finding an unknown side length, and exhibiting rectangles with the same perimeter and different areas or with the same area and different perimeters.	87–88
Geometry	
3.G.1. Understand that shapes in different categories (e.g., rhombuses, rectangles, and others) may share attributes (e.g., having four sides), and that the shared attributes can define a larger category (e.g., quadrilaterals). Recognize rhombuses, rectangles, and squares as examples of quadrilaterals, and draw examples of quadrilaterals that do not belong to any of these subcategories.	85–86, 89–90
3.G.2. Partition shapes into parts with equal areas. Express the area of each part as a unit fraction of the whole. *For example, partition a shape into 4 parts with equal area, and describe the area of each part as 1/4 of the area of the shape*	73–78

Answer Key

Test 1—Page 5
1. 4
2. 7
3. twenty-six
4. two hundred sixty-five
5. 902
6. 755
7. 767
8. 415
9. 297
10. 801

Test 2—Page 6
1. 7
2. 6
3. three hundred forty-six
4. eighty-nine
5. 841
6. 156
7. 205
8. 326
9. 406
10. 780

Test 3—Page 7
1. 5
2. 7
3. nine hundred ninety-six
4. eight hundred ninety-three
5. 932
6. 275
7. 123
8. 290
9. 49
10. 983

Test 4—Page 8
1. 1
2. 8
3. one thousand, nine hundred ninety-nine
4. three thousand, forty-eight
5. 2,567
6. 6,296
7. 2,618
8. 3,335
9. 1,269
10. 6,204

Test 5—Page 9
1. 3
2. 6
3. 4
4. 7
5. 5
6. 9
7. 305, 308, 405, 407
8. 223, 335, 352, 532
9. 987, 897, 798, 789
10. 218, 215, 181, 118

Test 6—Page 10
1. 365, 398, 437, 465
2. 342, 426, 635, 642
3. 603, 301, 205, 103
4. 211, 201, 121, 112
5. false
6. true
7. true
8. <
9. >
10. <

Test 7—Page 11
1. >
2. <
3. >
4. >
5. <
6. >
7. <
8. <
9. >
10. >

Test 8—Page 12
1. 22
2. 10
3. 24
4. 23
5. 21
6. 35
7. 32
8. 30
9. 28
10. 40

Test 9—Page 13
1. 25
2. 10
3. 22
4. 12
5. 45
6. 46
7. 58
8. 35
9. 26
10. 30

Test 10—Page 14
1. 18
2. 17
3. 12
4. 5 + 5 = 10; 10 + 2 = 12
5. 4 + 6 = 10; 10 + 5 = 15
6. 7 + 3 = 10; 10 + 9 = 19
7. 6 + 4 = 10; 10 + 5 = 15
8. 18 (circle 8, 2)
9. 19 (circle 7, 3)
10. 15 (circle 4, 6)

Test 11—Page 15
1. C
2. A
3. 10, 20, **30**, **40**, 50, **60**
4. 110, **120**, 130, **140**, 150, **160**
5. 90, **80**, **70**, 60, **50**, 40
6. **72**, 62, **52**, 42, **32**, 22
7. 20; 40
8. 45; 65
9. 73; 93
10. 12; 32

Test 12—Page 16
1. 1 hundred, 4 tens, 6 ones
2. 2 hundreds, 1 ten, 2 ones
3. 100, 200, **300**, **400**, 500, **600**, 700
4. **300**, **400**, 500, **600**, 700, **800**
5. 777, **677**, 577, **477**, 377, **277**
6. 600, **500**, 400, 300, **200**, **100**
7. 550; 750
8. 130; 330
9. 90; 290
10. 570; 770

Test 13—Page 17
1. 8, 10, 12, 14
2. 7, 9, 11, 13
3. 12, 15, 18, 21
4. 16, 20, 24, 28
5. 27, 29, 31, 33
6. each number is double the previous number
7. add 5 to each number
8. add 3 to each number
9. each number is half the previous number
10.

Test 14—Page 18
1. 999
2. 548
3. 863
4. 90 or ninety
5. 800 or eight hundred
6. 4 or four
7.
8.
9.
10.

Test 15—Page 19
1. 6,532
2. 4,321
3. 7,662
4. 9,852
5. 4,634, 4,433, 4,334, 4,246
6. 9,959, 9,695, 8,567, 7,765
7. 1,246, 1,467, 1,674, 1,764
8. 7,856, 7,865, 8,567, 8,765
9. 80 or eighty
10. 3,000 or three thousand

Test 16—Page 20
1. 2,432
2. 6,721
3. 8,467
4. 500 or five hundred
5. 8,000 or eight thousand
6. 20 or twenty
7. 6,367
8. 8,423
9. 5,647
10. 7,951 seven thousand, nine hundred fifty-one

Test 17—Page 21
1. 40 + 50 + 30 = 120
2. 60 + 60 + 50 = 170
3. 50 + 80 + 100 = 230
4. 73
5. 62
6. 95
7. 101
8. 81
9. 40 + **6** + **40** + 3 = 89
10. **60** + 6 + 30 + **3** = **99**

Test 18—Page 22

1. 27 + 25 + 32 = 84 eggs
2. 17 + 23 + 29 = 69 fish

3. ⑮

4	9	2
3	5	7
8	1	6

4. ㉝

14	9	10
7	11	15
12	13	8

5. ㊱

11	16	9
10	12	14
15	8	13

6. ㉑

6	11	4
5	7	9
10	3	8

7. 89
8. 98
9. $9.99
10. $6 89

Test 19—Page 23

1. 111
2. 92
3. 140
4. 910
5. 1,610
6. 1,042
7. 789 + 453 = 1,242
8. 47 + 74 = 121
9. 23 + 14 + 17 = 54
10. 32 + 48 + 59 = 139

Test 20—Page 24

1. 600
2. 1,000
3. 1,600
4. 19 (circle 6, 4)
5. 19 (circle 8, 2)
6. 17 (circle 5, 5)
7. >
8. <
9. 10 < 11
10. 16 = 16

Test 21—Page 25

1. 121
2. 110
3. 831
4. 1,410
5. 9,211
6. 9,127
7. 5
8. 8
9. 15 + 12 + 2 = 29
10. $350 + $85 = $435

Test 22—Page 26

1. 26
2. 12
3. 90
4. 168
5. 24
6. 110
7. 859
8. 6
9. 40
10. 35 + 17 = 52

Test 23—Page 27

1. 50
2. 7
3. 9
4. 4
5. 13
6. 2
7. 6
8. 8 – 6 = 2
9. 12 – 8 = 4
10. 16 – 10 = 6

Test 24—Page 28

1. 19 – 10 = 9
2. 15 – 10 = 5
3. 8
4. 9
5. 6
6. 10
7. 21 – 14 = 7; 21 – 7 = 14
8. 22 – 3 = 19; 22 – 19 = 3
9. $22 – $7 = $15
10. 100 – 56 = 44

Test 25—Page 29

1. 5
2. 4
3. 10 – 6 = 4
4. 11 – 4 = 7
5. 8 – 2 = 6
6. 12 – 6 = 6
7. 14 – 5 = 9
8. 9 – 0 = 9
9. 2
10. 6

Test 26—Page 30

1. 17 – 10 = 7
2. 17 – 15 = 2
3. 17 – 3 = 14
4. 17 – 12 = 5
5. 17 – 11 = 6
6. 17 – 5 = 12
7. 17 – 0 = 17
8. 17 – 7 = 10
9. 19 – 14 = 5
10. 14 – 5 = 9

Test 27—Page 31

1. 12 – 5 = 7
2. 16 – 7 = 9
3. 10 – 7 = 3
4. 14 – 6 = 8
5. 13 – 11 = 2
6. 5
7. 3
8. 9
9. 300
10. 25

Test 28—Page 32

1. 64
2. 13
3. 30
4. 11
5. 52
6. 55
7. 18
8. 12 – 3 = 9 or 12 – 9 = 3
9. 21 – 6 = 15 or 21 – 15 = 6
10. 18 – 12 = 6 or 18 – 6 = 12

Test 29—Page 33

1. 15
2. 29
3. 9
4.
$$\begin{array}{r} 65 \\ -29 \\ \hline 36 \end{array}$$
5.
$$\begin{array}{r} 98 \\ -47 \\ \hline 51 \end{array}$$
6.
$$\begin{array}{r} 68 \\ -49 \\ \hline 19 \end{array}$$
7.
$$\begin{array}{r} 57 \\ -28 \\ \hline 29 \end{array}$$
8. 86 – 62 = 24 or 86 – 24 = 62
9. 100 – 48 = 52 or 100 – 52 = 48
10. 85 – 48 = 37 marbles

Test 30—Page 34

1. 40 – 10 = 30
2. 14 – 8 = 6
3. 20 – 14 = 6
4. 36 – 18 = 18
5. 18 – 13 = 5
6. 50 – 23 = 27
7. 45 – 36 = 9
8. 67 – 48 = 19
9. 54 – 45 = 9
10. $99 – $42 = $57

Test 31—Page 35

1. 12
2. 17
3. 13
4. 25

5. ⊖

12	5	7
8	4	4
4	1	3

6. ⊖

20	13	7
6	4	2
14	9	5

7. ⊖

14	8	6
5	1	4
9	7	2

8. ⊖

33	22	11
17	8	9
16	14	2

9. ⊖

27	18	9
11	9	2
16	9	7

10. ⊖

20	9	11
10	3	7
10	6	4

Test 32—Page 36

1. 139
2. 411
3. 415
4. 142
5. 131
6. $900 – $850 = $50
7. $489 – $385 = $104
8. $46 – $32 = $14
9.
$$\begin{array}{r} 667 \\ -412 \\ \hline 255 \end{array}$$
10.
$$\begin{array}{r} 827 \\ -416 \\ \hline 411 \end{array}$$

Test 33—Page 37

1. 249
2. 274
3. 388
4. 78
5.
$$\begin{array}{r} 804 \\ -586 \\ \hline 218 \end{array}$$
6.
$$\begin{array}{r} 994 \\ -425 \\ \hline 569 \end{array}$$
7.
$$\begin{array}{r} 546 \\ -198 \\ \hline 348 \end{array}$$
8.
$$\begin{array}{r} 300 \\ -237 \\ \hline 63 \end{array}$$
9.
$$\begin{array}{r} \$495 \\ -168 \\ \hline \$327 \end{array}$$
10.
$$\begin{array}{r} \$853 \\ -674 \\ \hline \$179 \end{array}$$

Test 34—Page 38

1. 9
2. 25
3. 14
4. 19
5. 199
6. 9
7. 22
8. 50
9. $49 - 36 = 13$
10. $356 - 297 = 59$

Test 35—Page 39

1. 22
2. 16
3. 214
4. 189
5. $5.00 - $2.89 = $2.11
6–7. $20 - 7 = 13$ and $20 - 13 = 7$
8. Check answers.
9. Check answers.
10. Check answers.

Test 36—Page 40

1. $3 \times 5 = 15$ or $5 \times 3 = 15$
2. $7 \times 5 = 35$ or $5 \times 7 = 35$
3. $2 \times 9 = 18$ or $9 \times 2 = 18$
4. B. $8 \times 4 = 32$
5. true
6. false
7. true
8. variations of $6 \times 4 = 24$, $8 \times 3 = 24$, $2 \times 12 = 24$, or $1 \times 24 = 24$
9. variations of $6 \times 4 = 24$, $8 \times 3 = 24$, $2 \times 12 = 24$, or $1 \times 24 = 24$
10. variations of $6 \times 4 = 24$, $8 \times 3 = 24$, $2 \times 12 = 24$, or $1 \times 24 = 24$

Test 37—Page 41

1. 1, 2, 3, 6
2. 1, 17
3. 1, 3, 5, 15
4. 1, 2, 4, 8, 16
5. 18; $3 \times 6 = 18$
6. 49; $7 \times 7 = 49$
7. 45; $9 \times 5 = 45$
8. 6 groups of 6 equal 36
9. 9 groups of 2 equal 18
10. 4 groups of 10 equal 40

Test 38—Page 42

1. 35; 7
2. 12; 6
3. 24; 3
4. 63; 9
5. 36
6. 16
7. 25
8. true
9. true
10. false

Test 39—Page 43

1. $6 \times 7 = 42$
2. $6 \times 4 = 24$
3. 48
4. 24
5. 28
6. 45
7. 3
8. 3
9. 7
10. 7

Test 40—Page 44

1. 40
2. 55
3. 72
4. Possible answers: 3×8, 4×6, 2×12, 1×24
5. Possible answers: 3×4, 2×6, 1×12
6. Possible answers: 6×6, 4×9, 3×12, 2×18, 1×36
7. Possible answers: 5×8, 4×10, 2×20, 1×40
8. $.05 \times 7 = $.35$ or 5¢ x 7 = 35¢
9. $7 \times 7 = 49$
10. $2 \times 10 = 20$

Test 41—Page 45

1. 30
2. 36
3. 48
4. 28
5. 90
6. 40
7. 50
8. true
9. false
10. true

Test 42—Page 46

1. 63
2. 56
3. 32
4. $5 \times 12 = 60$ or $12 \times 5 = 60$
5. $4 \times 6 = 24$ or $6 \times 4 = 24$
6. $3 \times 12 = 36$ or $12 \times 3 = 36$
7. 11
8. 7
9. 5
10. 9

Test 43—Page 47

1. true
2. false
3. true
4. true
5. $6 \times 9 = 54$ or $9 \times 6 = 54$
6. $4 \times 7 = 28$ or $7 \times 4 = 28$
7. $9 \times 8 = 72$ or $8 \times 9 = 72$
8. 63
9. 64
10. 56

Test 44—Page 48

1–3. Possible answers: 6×6, 4×9, 3×12, 2×18, 1×36
4. 108
5. 48
6. 88
7. 9
8. 8
9. 3
10. 9

Test 45—Page 49

1. 55
2. 36
3. 35
4. 48
5. 8
6. 4
7. 2
8. $3 \times 6 = 18$
9. $2 \times 7 = 14$
10. $5 \times 10 = 50$

Test 46—Page 50

1. 9
2. 6
3. 5
4. 7
5. 7 groups of 4 = 28
6. 9 groups of 4 = 36
7. 10 groups of 4 = 40
8. >
9. =
10. <

Test 47—Page 51

1. 35
2. 49
3. 77
4. $9 \times 6 = 54$ and $6 \times 9 = 54$
5. $7 \times 9 = 63$ and $9 \times 7 = 63$
6. 28
7. 48
8. 36
9. false
10. true

Test 48—Page 52

1. 55
2. 24
3. 36
4. <
5. =
6. >
7. 4
8. 48
9. 7, 8
10. $4 \times 7 = 28$

Test 49—Page 53

1. 5 groups of 2 or $10 \div 2 = 5$
2. 5 groups of 4 or $20 \div 4 = 5$
3. 5 groups of 3 or $15 \div 3 = 5$
4. 3
5. 2
6. 6
7. 9
8. $24 \div 3 = 8$
9. $24 \div 12 = 2$
10. $24 \div 4 = 6$

Test 50—Page 54

1. 7
2. 10
3. 9
4. 4
5. 10
6. 6
7. 2
8. 7
9. 7
10. 6

Test 51—Page 55

1. $8 \div 2 = 4$; $8 \div 4 = 2$
2. $14 \div 2 = 7$; $14 \div 7 = 2$
3. $12 \div 4 = 3$; $12 \div 3 = 4$
4. 3
5. 2
6. 2
7. 5
8. 5
9. 42
10. 7

Test 52—Page 56

1. $6 \div 2 = 3$; $6 \div 3 = 2$
2. $18 \div 3 = 6$; $18 \div 6 = 3$
3. $24 \div 6 = 4$; $24 \div 4 = 6$
4. $32 \div 4 = 8$; $32 \div 8 = 4$
5. 10
6. 7
7. 6 cupcakes
8. 4 cupcakes
9. 3 cupcakes
10. 9 cupcakes

Test 53—Page 57

1. 4
2. 3
3. 6
4. 2
5. 3

6. 4
7. 3
8. 3
9. 8
10. 7

Test 54—Page 58

1. 6
2. 5
3. 7
4. 9
5. 35

6. 6
7. 6
8. 15 ÷ 5 = 3; 15 ÷ 3 = 5
9. 28 ÷ 4 = 7; 28 ÷ 7 = 4
10. 30 ÷ 5 = 6; 30 ÷ 6 = 5

Test 55—Page 59

1. 6
2. 12
3. 4
4. 8
5. 3

6. 3
7. 4
8. 4; 16 ÷ 4 = 4
9. 4; 32 ÷ 8 = 4
10. 5; 45 ÷ 9 = 5

Test 56—Page 60

1. 3
2. 8
3. 9
4. 9
5. 20

6. 9
7. 6
8. 9
9. 5
10. 7

Test 57—Page 61

1. 4
2. 3
3. 2
4. 5
5. 8

6. 4
7. 7
8. 4
9. 6
10. 7

Test 58—Page 62

1. 5
2. 36
3. 8
4. 4
5. 3

6. 4
7. 7
8. 8
9. 40 ÷ 8 = 5
10. 33 ÷ 3 = 11

Test 59—Page 63

1. 3
2. 6
3. 9
4. 36
5. 12 ÷ 3 = 4

6. 12 ÷ 6 = 2
7. 12 ÷ 4 = 3
8. 4; 16 ÷ 4 = 4
9. 5; 30 ÷ 6 = 5
10. 5; 35 ÷ 7 = 5

Test 60—Page 64

1. 9
2. 9
3. 10
4. 8
5. 5; 20 ÷ 4 = 5

6. 6; 36 ÷ 6 = 6
7. 2; 18 ÷ 9 = 2
8. 9
9. 9
10. 45

Test 61—Page 65

1. 40 ÷ 5 = 8
2. 100 ÷ 10 = 10
3. 6
4. 7
5. 5

6. 3
7. 7
8. 3
9. 3
10. 5

Test 62—Page 66

1. 24 ÷ 3 = 8
2. 54 ÷ 9 = 6
3. 4
4. 3
5. 35

6. 7
7. 4 x 10 = 40
8. 4
9. 4 *remainder* 4
10. 5 *remainder* 5

Test 63—Page 67

1. 3
2. 2
3. 4 *remainder* 2
4. 2 *remainder* 4
5. 5 *remainder* 1

6. 5 *remainder* 7
7. 6 *remainder* 3
8. 5 *remainder* 2
9. 28 ÷ 6 = 4 r.4
10. 20 ÷ 6 = 3 r.2

Test 64—Page 68

1. 2 *remainder* 1
2. 2 *remainder* 6
3. 4 *remainder* 2
4. 3 *remainder* 1
5. 3 *remainder* 3; 4 houses

6. 3
7. 3
8. 17 ÷ 5 = 3 *remainder* 2
9. 3
10. 2

Test 65—Page 69

1. 80
2. 61
3. 56
4. 4
5. 5; 5

6. 6; 6
7. 11; 11
8. 6; 6
9. 5 x 4 = 20 Multiplication
10. 16 ÷ 4 = 4 Division

Test 66—Page 70

1. 66
2. 65
3. 35
4. 44
5. 60
6. 4
7. 5
8. 27
9. 21 + 12 + 38 = 71 Addition
10. 3 x 5 = 15 Multiplication

Test 67—Page 71

1. 4 *remainder* 2
2. 4 *remainder* 2
3. 4 *remainder* 3
4. 32
5. 60

6. 28
7. 34
8. 46
9. 13 – 7 = 6 Subtraction
10. 5 x 3 = 15 Multiplication

Test 68—Page 72

1. 12
2. 35
3. 2
4. 1 *remainder* 2
5. ÷

6. ×
7. 104
8. 29
9. 20 ÷ 10 = 2 Division
10. 25 – 8 = 17 Subtraction

Test 69—Page 73

1. 6 x 25 = 150 $1.50
2. 8 x 1 = 8   8¢ or .08
3. 6 x 5 = 30   30¢ or .30
4. 9 x 10 = 90   90¢ or .90
5. 80¢
6. $1.00
7. $2.00
8. 40¢
9. $4.00 x 3 = $ 12.00
10. $80 ÷ 8 = $10.00

Test 70—Page 74

1. 3 × $3.00 = $9.00
2. 8 × $3.00 = $24.00
3. 5 × $3.00 = $15.00
4. $1.55
5. $0.77 or 77¢
6. $1.65
7. $2.00 + $1.75 = $3.75
8. $3.50 + $1.50 = $5.00
9. $2.00 + $1.50 = $3.50
10. $1.75 + $1.50 = $3.25

Answer Key (cont.)

Test 71—Page 75
1. 6 × 9 = 54
2. 4 × 9 = 36
3. 9 × 9 = 81
4. $3.25 + $2.50 = $5.75
5. $4.75 + $.50 + $.50 = $5.75
6. $3.25 + $3.25 + $.75 = $7.25
7. $2.50 + $.75 = $3.25
8. $3.00
9. $3.85
10. $2.90

Test 72—Page 76
1. 4 x 50¢ = $2.00
2. 6 x 50¢ = $3.00
3. 8 x 50¢ = $4.00
4. 10 x 50¢ = $5.00
5. 3 x 50¢ = $1.50
6. $55 + $55 = $110.00
7. $102 + $39 = $141.00
8. 5 quarters
9. 15 nickels
10. 35 pennies

Test 73—Page 77
1. one half
2. one quarter
3. two thirds
4. Variations of
5. Variations of
6. Variations of
7. 2/4
8. 6/8
9. 4/6
10. 4/8

Test 74—Page 78
1. 2
2. 3
3. 2
4. 1/2
5. 3/4
6. 2/4 or 1/2
7. 6/8 or 3/4
8. =
9. >
10. =

Test 75—Page 79
1. 3/4
2. 1/2
3. 3/6
4. 6/8
5. 2/4
6. 6/6
7. 2/3
8. 2/6 or 1/3
9. 4/8 or 1/2
10. 3/6 or 1/2

Test 76—Page 80
1–3. Answers will be variations of shading shown.

1. 2. 3.

4. 1/3
5. 2/8
6. 5/8
7. 1/8, 2/8, 7/8, 8/8
8. show three ladybugs circled
9. 7/8
10. 1/6

Test 77—Page 81
1. D
2. C
3. B
4. A
5. 4/8
6. 5/8
7. = (Check shading.)
8. > (Check shading.)
9. > (Check shading.)
10. = (Check shading.)

Test 78—Page 82
1.
2.
3.
4.
5.
6. 2
7. 2
8. 4
9. 1
10. 5

Test 79—Page 83
1. 6:30
2. 3:20
3. 1:05
4. 10:45
5. true
6. true
7. false
8. true
9. 3:00
10. 4:15

Test 80—Page 84
1. 2:30
2. 12:00
3. 9:15
4.   5.   6.
7. 2:45
8. 11:30
9. 8:15
10. 12:45

Test 81—Page 85
1. D
2. C
3. A
4. B
5. 2:30
6. 11:00
7. 3:45
8. 9:15
9. 5:00
10. 3:30

Test 82—Page 86
1. 1:10
2. 12:20
3. 8:40
4.   5.   6.
7. 4:50
8. 9:10
9. 7:15
10. 12:00

Test 83—Page 87
1. 12:15
2. 3:30
3. 4:45
4. 10:00
5. false
6. true
7. true
8. false
9. 7:00
10. 9:45

Test 84—Page 88
1. 2 and a half hours
2. 9:45
3. 4:00
4. 4:30
5. 1:20
6. 3:30
7. 4:30
8. 5:15
9. 11:25
10. 10:50

Test 85—Page 89
1. triangle
2. oval
3. rhombus
4. square
5. Octagon should be circled.
6. Oval should be circled.
7. Triangle should be circled.
8. C
9. B
10. C

Test 86—Page 90
1. 4
2. 3
3. no
4. 5
5. 4
6. 8
7. 6

8.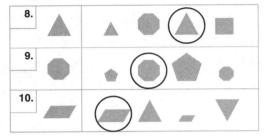

9.

10.

Test 87—Page 91
1. 13
2. 20
3. 6
4. 6
5. 7
6. 9
7. 16
8. 16
9. false
10. true

Test 88—Page 92
1. 18 in.
2. 14 in.
3. 20 in.
4. true
5. true
6. false
7. 3 cm
8. 4 cm
9. 60 feet
10. 12 feet

Test 89—Page 93
1. cube
2. cylinder
3. cone
4. sphere
5. prism
6. A
7. C
8. A
9. B
10. D

Test 90—Page 94
1. sphere
2. rectangular prism
3. cone
4. cube
5. 5
6. 6
7. 6
8. square   rectangle
9. triangle   rectangle
10. 8

Test 91—Page 95
1. inches²
2. yards²
3. yards²
4. inches²
5. 16
6. 12
7. 4
8. 4
9. 5
10. 6

Test 92—Page 96
1. 64
2. 45
3. 21
4. 8
5. yes
6. 7
7. 8
8. 10
9. inches²
10. yards²

Test 93—Page 97
1. B
2. C
3. A
4. 6 pints
5. 10 pints
6. 8 quarts
7. 16 quarts
8. pool
9. teaspoon
10. bucket

Test 94—Page 98
1. 25 grams
2. 2 kilograms
3. 2 grams
4. 1 kilogram
5. 2,000
6. A
7. B
8. E
9. B
10. yes

Test 95—Page 99
1. 12
2. 3
3. 36
4. 2
5. 4
6. 5
7. 36
8. 72
9. $59 \div 12 = 4r.11$ 4 feet 11 inches
10. $28 \div 12 = 2r.4$ 2 feet 4 inches

Test 96—Page 100
1. 1 inch
2. 1 ½ inches
3. 2 ½ inches
4. 24
5. 48
6. 72
7. 6
8. 30
9. 6; $3 \times 2 = 6$
10. 36; $6 \times 6 = 36$

Test 97—Page 101
1. D
2. 85°F
3. B
4. 50°F
5. Check thermometer.
6. Check thermometer.
7. Check thermometer.
8. Check thermometer.
9. 40°
10. 20°

Test 98—Page 102
1. thermometer
2. measuring tape
3. measuring cup
4. scale
5. inches
6. pounds
7. ounces
8. 32
9. 16
10. one pound

Test 99—Page 103
1. soccer
2. hockey
3. 15 votes
4. swimming and football
5. bus
6. walk
7. bike and car
8. red
9. white
10. red

Test 100—Page 104
1. ice cream
2. cupcakes
3. candy and donuts
4. brown
5. Hazel
6. $10 - 3 = 7$
7. green and blue
8. $9 + 7 = 16$
9. Jett
10. Jeff